Let That Shit Go

Learn to Process Loss and Be Happy

Teachings of Rose

JOANNE HELFRICH

NewWorldView
Topanga, California

NewWorldView
Topanga, California
newworldview.com

The Way of Spirit: Teachings of Rose
thewayofspirit.com

First Printing: July 2018
ISBN: 978-0-9828123-5-8

Printed in the United States on acid-free, partially recycled paper.
10 9 8 7 6 5 4 3 2 1.1

— CONTENTS —

for Erin

Foreword

Welcome to this wonderful little book. I didn't write it—spirit guides did—so my first experience reading it was a lot like yours now. It has helped me to be a much happier person, and I trust it will help you, too.

The reason I say "spirit guides" wrote it is to give them the credit they deserve (more about this in a bit), but the inception of this book came from my lifelong struggle with anxiety and depression. Like you, perhaps, my frustration has grown with every suicide, sorrow, and side effect experienced by people I've known and many I haven't.

Despite the many advances in modern science, there are more depressed and suicidal people today than ever. The prevailing assumption is that mental illness is incurable and we can only manage it through medication. Certainly, medication can help, but most often only temporarily. The assumption that there is no cure prevents us from having any hope for healing.

Modern science's shortcomings are the result of the limited perspective that denies the spiritual reality that we are part of. The perspectives of spiritual teachers and mystics are far more accurate and useful. So useful, in fact, that *the people who become healed of their mental and emotional distress are those who include a spiritual dimension in their therapy.*

The central premises of authentic spiritual sources are that we are spiritual beings who create our physical reality for our own experiences, that life continues beyond it, that we are eternally loved, and that there are always spiritual guides near us who want to help.

This is not something we might ever prove using modern methods, or must take on faith, but is something *we directly experience when we open to it.* Teachers and therapists can be greatly helpful, but ultimately it's up to us to find what we need inside ourselves and translate it into our lives in ways that benefit us and others, too.

Everyone has the ability to tune into their inner spiritual reality and accurately "channel" inner experience and knowledge through expressions in their everyday lives. I claim this with all sincerity because my experience proves it to me daily.

My form of channeling inner knowledge happens in many ways, most notably through my writing and speaking. I receive "downloads" from spirit through my kinesthetic sense while "autotyping" with a keyboard or without one, as I'm also able to comprehend and speak what comes through me.

FOREWORD

I consider my ability one of the many kinds of exceptional abilities people have, just more unusual than most. I believe everyone has these sorts of "superpowers" whether or not they recognize them, or recognize them for the amazing abilities that they are.

It's always with a great dose of discernment that I allow these spirit guides to speak through me, and I encourage everyone to be discerning, too.

Who are they, and what are their intentions?

If you consider that life continues in some energetic form after our physical bodies expire, it stands to reason that we, and all individuals, continue to grow — to evolve — in nonphysical reality. We can consider the spirits who wrote this book as highly evolved. They know what it's like to be human, they've done the work to evolve, and they want to show us how to do that, too.

The spirit guides who entrust me with their work call themselves Rose. We refer to "her" as a "she," but "she" is actually a "we" (the result of the limitations of our language, especially pronouns!). We can think of Rose as a wide, loving, nonphysical energy collective who can help us open up to who we are: multidimensional selves that are much bigger than we imagine, and include big spiritual energies like her.

Rose helps us realize our direct connection with our essence — our Personal God — by embracing what she calls our *way of spirit*, and in doing so, live our most fulfilling lives. You can find out more about your way of spirit in this book and in Rose's foundational work, *The Way of Spirit: Teachings of Rose*. You can find out more about Rose at *thewayofspirit.com*.

Ultimately, the important thing is the value of the information in our lives, not where it comes from.

No matter what the source, the cure requires us to do the deep and challenging inner spiritual work.

This book will guide you, and it will be worth it. As the first recipient of its magic, I know.

Now it is in your hands!

\- Joanne Helfrich
Topanga, California

Introduction

When you are in love, you feel wonderful. You sense around you the pulse of love in everything. The trees take on magical qualities. The birds sing only for you.

This is how life should feel. Indeed, this is how life should feel even when you are not in love, for love is merely the anticipation that the things that come your way will all be good.

Doing the work to get past beliefs that hold
you back from the feelings of love in your life
has to do with the process of grieving.

The losses you've encountered in your life have all, to some degree, been the means to allow yourself to be different than you were before.

However, many times you may not have been aware that the loss was necessary, so you held onto who you thought you needed to be. But loss always has some benefit, and there are ways to grieve loss that can restore your life in beautiful ways.

This is what the book will help you do:
to feel that the world will give you what you need,
in spite of what you think.

In this, the losses you've encountered—that you've needed to let go of and grieve—will help you determine the course of your life in the future without need to feel that the past has been anything but purposeful.

The goal of this book, therefore, is to help you be who you were born to be without fear of loss, or need to grieve without ceasing, for the world is not the same world you've been raised to believe it is.

The world is a place of great beauty. You just need to see it this way again.

Chapter 1: Know
that Love Rules

There's no better word for *life* than *love*. When you stop to really consider it, love really does rule.

You see this in your expressions of love for each other in everyday life with the people you know. Strangers do great acts of kindness for one another, too.

The path of love even seems to always be the right path for you to follow in your intellectual capacity to realize how life should be.

However, in love there are always challenges.

The best way to define *love* may be *the ability to realize your greater Self—your essence Self, your Personal God—in every moment.*

This is a very different sort of definition than you've come to find so far. However, isn't love exactly what expresses itself when you think higher thoughts, words, deeds, and actions? In expressing your essence Self, you get the best of love, do you not?

The way to describe this sort of love is *capturing the best self in order to work through the times that are not always sunshine and flowers.*

You have to sometimes work at loving, and thinking about your essence Self's ability to look upon all things with compassion will not help you all the time. In this, feeling that you are in love will only get you so far, too, as love is not always about pain-free life. Love is often about sorrow and misery.

In this, you can expect the path to be broken into bits as you care for people who do not respond to your love, or who take actions that seem to cause pain to the people you love, or who, despite everything, seem to just have bad luck. These ways of spirit have reason to be also.

Everyone follows a different path

Now, if you have read our previous book, *The Way of Spirit*, you will see that everybody has his or her own path to follow. In this, everybody is not going to follow the same path. Some, in fact, will not realize their own calling, their way of spirit. In this, it's simply a case of not realizing the best self they were born to realize.

It's important to understand that every person who has ever been born has had some tough times, some so great they have not lived for very long, for example. In this, every path must be honored, whether it is for naught in the sense of achievement or deep satisfaction.

KNOW THAT LOVE RULES

The paths of every individual are expressions of Godhood whether you think of them that way or not. In this, self-respect, orderliness, consideration for others, and the many qualities that you may think of as refined or good have absolutely no bearing on the value of a human life.

Do you follow? There are no rules when it comes to what each individual has reason to express in their lives.

In this, the satisfaction of knowing you did a good job in your life goes right out the window, doesn't it? The respect, values, sense of achievement, and other means of categorizing events in one's life are all now put into a category called "judgment" that we will say has no bearing on the actual value of an individual life.

Now, that said, some things are worth inferring as good or bad. Pain is bad. Non-pain is good. Non-pain is also a way to think about how you often try to express only the best things in life. But believing that life is not supposed to include pain or sorrow is not helpful to you. It is the perfection belief at work, as well as thinking that you are supposed to be better or worse.

So the first order of business that we suggest is needed to realign your thoughts about life is this:

Don't think that life is supposed to be pain-free.
This is the perfection belief at work.
Don't let it rule your life.

In this, the perfection belief that you have is not grounded in any deep spiritual teaching. Think about this: what spiritual teaching has ever taught you to be perfect? Indeed, most individuals have never even been taught this explicitly.

The only reason people believe in perfection is that they believe it will spare them from pain.

So don't believe that you are supposed to be perfect. The fact is, you will never be perfect, even in your most advanced stages of development.

The path for you is about being happy.

In this, the love you have for self is the most important thing you can find to help you do that.

In this, love really does rule, as we've said. When you see how the world really does exist in a glorious state of love, you will forget all about your ideas about perfection. The world is not perfect, neither are any potential futures that we spirits can find for your world. However, the world is full of many sorts of love, and in your ability to see this is where the joy comes in.

The world is not a great big ball of pain as your respectable news reports sometimes tell you. The world is more of a place to realize that pain is part of life—as well as love—sometimes.

There's only reason to *gain* love when you see the news, not *lose* love. In this, when you look at the news and other things such as scientific reports of the doom ahead, you need to realize that *life really does want to end well.*

It's not that individuals are trying to scare you, it's that they are the ones who are scared. They trust only the material world for answers, and believe that life is a series of random and chaotic events. They have tuned out much of their *spiritual sense* in order to think they are in control.

But if you use your spiritual sense to perceive the loving connectedness of all things, you will know that all of life is purposeful, and that it cannot end badly for you.

Everything you do has purpose

Do you follow? Every one of your sad feelings, your pain—and even your lack of feelings about what makes you sad—has purpose. What more can you want from life than to let go of what you can't control?

In this, the news provides an actual service because you can say, "Okay. What can I do to help this situation? What can I do to let go of what I can't control or do to help?"

Therefore, the news gives you a marvelous way to learn to let go of some things and turn them over to spiritual beings who have your back in any case. So do so. We'll talk more about this a bit later.

Now, how you get by on having so much fear in you is a wonder to us, because you have way too much fear to really be happy. In this, love is the answer.

When you realize that the future is fine, you get a sense of being in love again. Do you realize how many individuals are unhappy just because they fear the future? Do you understand that they would be happy if they just didn't fear so much?

For when you are in love, what do you think about? You think about all the wonderful times ahead with the person you love. You think about the exciting things too, perhaps, the sex, the drama even. *You get a sense the world is really looking out after you.*

In this, you manage to have the joy back that you did not have for the time you spent being fearful of life and of the future.

So being in love is perhaps the best feeling in the world, and who better than you to feel that way again?

Do you see how being "over-the-moon in love" can transform the world?
Starting with you?

Now, we will also say that the world has many reasons to be serious. What more can one do than to be serious about subjects like hunger or war-stricken areas that so many individuals are stuck in, wanting your help?

You can help by being happy. This does not mean that you must take on everything with a sense of not caring. *You need to care.* However, there's only so much you can do to help sometimes.

KNOW THAT LOVE RULES

In this, you must realize that each individual has his or her own way of spirit to follow, and sometimes the path has included—and must include—pain. There is nothing you can do sometimes. There are always ways you can be a better person. That's what the images on television are trying to tell you: what can you do to be a better person?

Now, in your history you have found many reasons to act with great force. The world wars are examples of how you have responded to threats from the many resource-heavy countries who want to project their pain onto you and the rest of the world.

In this, you have reason to push back sometimes, yes you do. However, in your pushing back is what? Love. Yes. This is hard for you to grasp because you've been taught that aggression is bad or wrong, but aggression can sometimes be love in force.

The aggression of the world is not something to fear, but is something to realize has good and bad reasons for being. We are deliberately using the words *good* and *bad* so you can think about them differently, not to express an absolute judgment on anyone or any action.

The expressions of "good" and "bad" sometimes need saying, and when you do, realize that these are judgments, that's all. Lack of judgment too often falls into the areas of *lacking discernment* when used to project shadow, which we will discuss.

For now, try to realize that good and bad have reasons to be held as ideas.

The world is you

When the world is happy, you want to sing along. When you have a hurt, you want to heal it. When you see the world hurting, you want to heal that, too. If you feel bad, sometimes you want the world to feel bad, too.

Why? Because you are the world, really.

The world is you. It is a projection of your essence Self. When the world hurts, you hurt, because you are the same thing. To deny how you feel when the world hurts—perhaps by rationalizing that you can't take the hurt—is not helpful. You need to fully realize your connection with the world.

However, this does not mean that you have control over the world. In fact, the part of you that does *not* have control has been wanting to get your attention for a very long time. The world aches for you to realize how to be happy in spite of the sorrows.

In this, you need to deal with your sorrows, and what better way to do so than the grief process? We will switch topics now because we want to express to you how very much you need to learn to grieve.

Chapter 2:
Learn to Grieve

Grief is a byproduct of sorrow and loss. It is a function of the soul more than the mind, although the mind provides an important layer of required analysis to help you understand the reasons for your sorrow or loss.

Your many reasons for grief have left you somewhat bankrupt of feeling because you have not known how to process your sorrow and loss. In fact, you have barely recognized some sorrow and loss because you have not been taught to do so. You have been taught to only win.

Haven't the reasons for winning been tied to perfection as well? The perfect self thinks there's not any reason to lose or to admit defeat. This is perhaps the most damaging belief there is, for in not identifying loss, you have realized significant sorrow, but internalized and sublimated it.

This is why so very many of you are depressed.

Most people living in the so-called
civilized parts of the world are so cut off
from their sorrow they don't know what
to do except to medicate themselves.

This is making things worse in every way, because it is piling up sorrow upon sorrow *without an opportunity to release it.*

Therefore, the first step in the grief process is simply to acknowledge your loss.

Step 1: Acknowledge your loss

One, you realize that something is changed. It may not be anything big. Perhaps someone has stolen your pencil. Let's say you are a small child, and this would cause you a lot of pain, given how much you feel out of control of things already.

The person who has stolen your pencil may not even be aware of the pain he or she has caused you. However, the pain is there for you.

You believe that the pencil is supposed to be a good thing to have. Now, maybe it is and maybe it isn't. Perhaps the pencil doesn't have any special qualities, but it was your pencil, dammit. The pencil was yours and it is wrong to steal. You have a sense the pencil has trusted you with it, perhaps, and do not want to feel that you have done something wrong. All these things that come to mind are welling in your throat as you realize that you have lost your glorious pencil.

Now, we are not suggesting that it is wrong that the loss of the pencil would make you feel this way. You have many things that you hold dear, like the pencil you had as a child that may have been stolen.

This is not just a pencil: *it is a representation of everything that you think of as good.*

Pay attention to your shadow

Now, in adoring what you love, you sometimes let yourself move into areas of shadow. The shadow is your self who helps you realize things that you need to understand.

When you attach reasons for feeling good about yourself to things you love, that's the shadow at work.

The shadow will point out the things that are truly in need of realizing. For example, the pencil represents that you are good, trustworthy, and capable of writing things.

The same goes for anything that you find dear. Perhaps it is how you bake a pie. If someone were to come along and say your pie tastes terrible, you would feel totally despairing. That's because you have put your self-worth into the pie-making, not into yourself.

Do you follow? The shadow will help you realize that you are not the pie-making. You are not the pencil. Your value is not in what you have or how you do things. *Your value is in who you are.*

Back to the pencil scenario. When you think about what the pencil represents to you, you get a feeling that you need to really *let that shit go.* We mean *shit,* too, because your ideas about you having to be better is the point.

That is the exact shit that makes flowers grow.

In your grief, then, are the flowers of your potential outcomes, which are attainable by fully embracing the process to get to where you need to be.

The world will summon all its power to help you see the future as better than what you have now. In this, you will get a sense of joy again.

However, going through the process can be terrible. It is hard losing something that you love. It is worse losing *someone* that you love. But in this, the magic will express repeatedly how you can move through this in ways that are truly miraculous.

Say you aspire to being a better musician. You get better and better each time you practice. The same goes for the grief process. Each time you learn to work through it, you get better at it. Then you make it more of a habit, not just something that you do when someone dies.

Do you see how necessary it is to lie down every night and feel that you have won something? And in the *winning* you have realized that it's because you really did *lose* something?

> *That's the key to realizing the grief process:*
> *you find the wins in the losses.*

The purpose to love, as we said, is sometimes to let go of how you think about your future. And love is more than this, but we will focus on this small part now because it opens the door to almost everything there is to know about love.

Feel the pull of love into the future

The love you feel when you are in love draws you into the future in multiple ways. It strengthens you for your daily activities. It helps you project feelings of newness. It moves you into thinking about fine, beautiful things that may or may not happen, but feel wonderful to daydream about.

> *That's what is needed when you grieve:*
> *the pull of love into the future.*

The future is going to be fine in any case, whether you see it this way or not, because eventually spirit will come into the picture. In the most severe cases, if you are trapped in grief, you will often decide to no longer be physical. When that occurs, the spiritual being that you are—your essence—will help you sort out your challenges and move into new areas of expression.

Now, it's also important to note that you will need to work on your challenges in any case, living or not. In this, you can cross suicide off your list of potential helpful things, because if you think this will solve your problems, *it will not.*

> *Suicide only makes you nonphysical:*
> *it does not allow you to realize*
> *a future without problems.*

You go as you when you die, and there's not any reason to fear this. However, you will not let go of your challenges, because these are part of your development as a human being, even when you're dead.

Do you realize how important this grief process is? *It's so very important that you will not escape it, even if you die.*

So let's continue with the process, because this is perhaps the most important thing you can learn right now.

> *If you are suffering, it's always*
> *because of the shadow.*

The shadow plays with your thoughts and fears to such a large degree that you don't even realize it sometimes. The shadow will say what you need to be doing and feeling because of *the fears you have*, not because of *the loss you feel*.

There's a difference between letting go of one pencil and thinking that the pencil represents how your mother felt about you when she gave you the pencil. Your mother, if she's a good mother, will love you no matter what. Yet you attach to your pencil everything that you *believe* you should be for your mother to love you.

This is the heart of the matter: the groomed, well behaved child is the most susceptible to depression because of the expectations he or she has to be a good little boy or girl.

When this sort of loss occurs, it's heartbreaking because so much is riding on the success of their everyday school life—their admissions tests, their performance in grade school—that they have missed the boat with regard to what really makes them happy. And in this, the antidepressants go a long way to dull down the fears and feelings of hopelessness that are caused by these seemingly small and insignificant actions that occur every day.

The pencils are just the beginning. When you grow older, you have more than pencils weighing you down. You have principals and teachers who don't like you for some reason, you have loss of face after losing a big game, you have loss of friendships, sometimes for no good reason, as is often the case in elementary and middle school.

All these hurts are not processed, they are sublimated. And when you get to college, by then you are so riddled with loss that your only choices seem to be to take the easy path through whatever you aspire to doing: get the job, get a mortgage, and take no risks, period.

Get the insurance policy so that you are never fearful again, nor will you lose, when life is all about loss, dear ones... always!

The way out of this, as we said, is to grieve.

Step 2: Use your fears to take action

When we last left our little boy, he had lost the dearest thing he could imagine in the moment, and isn't that how it always feels? It doesn't matter if the thing was large or small. Losing is tough. So when he sees the pencil in the hand of another child, he doesn't know what to do, or perhaps he takes action.

In this, the actions are important. When you have something taken from you, what do you do? You want to tear something apart. This is a natural instinct. The fear makes you want to take action, and this is what fear is for.

Fear is about taking action,
not continuing to fear.

So in the course of the day's events, when you lose something, you fear. You want to take action. If you do take action, great, if not, that's a choice. However, if you don't act, you sometimes miss the boat, and fear piles on top of fear, and then you have anxiety.

So in this case, the pencil needs to be rescued from the hand of the perpetrator. How? Through force, perhaps, or by telling the teacher, or by stealing it back when they aren't looking. These are all viable options. However, they may not all be the best.

The point is (pardon the pun) that the fear is to take action. If the action is not taken, the fear will continue, then worry about why you did not act.

Now, sometimes the loss is too great to take in, much less recognize there's fear involved. An example of this is if you have lost a loved one tragically. The fear may be in getting them to the hospital to make sure they get the treatment they need, given there was an opportunity to do so. So in the *potential* loss, when the action was in process, there may have been reason to move into new areas of expression to prevent the loss. This is where bargaining comes in.

Step 3: Acknowledge what you could have done better

You have heard the word *bargaining* in the grief process to describe something that we will define as *the act of ensuring you can do better next time.*

Bargaining is not the best word, so we will use the words *accessing alternatives,* for it is in accessing what you think you could have done better that is the most important part about grief, as it attends to the response you have and the future you will bring about as a result of your loss.[1]

The best self knows what you could do better in any situation, whether it is in finding and gaining back your pencil, in attending to your loved one who needs you, or perhaps in embracing the fact that your worth is not contingent on how your mother feels about you, for example.

These are hugely important processes to go through. Sometimes these processes need the intervention of a good spiritual guide, teacher, or therapist. In every case, though, there's probably something you could have done better. That's the heart of the matter.

If you can realize what that thing was, forgive yourself for it, and move on, taking action if you need to, then you have discovered the flowers that grow in grief, because no one is served if nothing good comes from it.

This is important to do.

Now, when you grieve, you have reason to also move past what you have lost into another self. This is because

---

[1] See the *Access Alternatives* practice on page 130.

you have attached something of yourself to the thing or person that you lost. It's as if something was lost that once was a part of you.

However, the thing that was lost was not only a part of you, it is *still* a part of you. So you must separate what *is* a part of you from what *is not* a part of you. This is the tricky part.

When you lose something fairly small, like a pencil, you gather that you have no reason to feel badly about it when you consider it was only a pencil. Perhaps you have realized that the pencil wasn't as important as you thought, and does not command your mother's love, as you may have thought it does.

Now, what value is there to that? Well, everything! A mother's love is not contingent on the pencil. Therefore, perhaps if your mother's love is contingent on the pencil, you can let go of the need to please your mother so much. Or you can let go of the need to sympathize too greatly with those who worry too much about losing their pencils. Indeed, if you don't really need to carry the sympathy for others who carry pencils with so much weight, then why do it?

Compassion, not sympathy, moves you into new areas of expression

We are using the word *sympathize* not meaning to be the same as *have compassion for*. These are totally different things. Sympathy can have negative affects if taken too far—for example, if you are not moving from the areas of sympathy into new areas of expression.

In this, the *compassion* you feel for self when you lose something is much more beneficial than having *sympathy* for yourself, because sympathy does not move you into new areas of expression the way compassion does.

We suggest, too, that in your perception about sympathy are many fears. The sympathy for others that occurs when loss is attained is wholesome and good. The past is moving into the future and you can feel sympathy for others when they are grieving.

However, to carry on with sympathy after the time of mourning is over is not always healthy, and may cause more harm than good if you have reason to expect that your sympathy for others will only saddle them with more of the non-helpful responses to grief than they'd have if you didn't. They may not care much about meaningful dialog with essence about how they can change.

Sometimes people need to be encouraged to move on. The same goes for you after you have done the process of grieving.

Step 4: Let go

The letting go is not always easy. The path for you has been fraught with the idea that you can "take it with you".

However, you know there are many reasons to let go of things. In fact, the more you let go of, the happier you are, typically. This is different from loss: it's the process that occurs after the loss as been acknowledged and accepted by allowing yourself to understand where you could be a better person, as well as happy person, in spite of—or better yet, because of—the loss.

So let's go back to our scenario. You've lost your pencil, the one your mother gave you. You have fear that there were things in your control that you needed to act on. Perhaps you got the pencil back by claiming it was stolen, when in reality the pencil was on the floor and somebody took it by mistake.

Now what do you do? You can see how your shadow was at work because of the fear you had of losing face with your mother, or even losing her love. The shadow took over and blamed somebody else for your misery.

See how that works? So you have been handed back your pencil and you see how you were wrong about how you handled it. This is still a loss of face, of pride, of belief in your right-ness.

Is this such a bad thing to realize? Not if you have enough fortitude to see that you really didn't mean to do anything wrong, that you strive to be a better person, and that your mother will love you no matter what.

How is this now a loss? It's not. It's an opportunity to be a better person, to think of yourself differently. In this, love pulls you into the letting go phase.

Now, in order to move forward, you need to have achieved the first steps: acknowledge the loss, use your fears to take action, see what you could have done or can do better, and acknowledge what you learned from the experience so you can let go.

Then the way to move into new areas of expression is to find new strength in your new self.

Chapter 3: Claim
Your New Self

What a beautiful thing to consider, that grief is all about finding out how to move into new areas of expression!

How wonderful to claim a new self who is less likely to fear, less likely to feel badly about himself, and less likely to be traumatized by loss in the future!

In this, your spiritual sense has bearing on how to move forward. This is often lost in your psychiatric practice because many of the people who are running the show do not have a spiritual component, but in the future, they will. For now, it is up to you to strengthen yourselves spiritually so you can move into new areas of expression and take in what you can to claim *who you have signed up to be in this lifetime*—to claim your *intent*.

Because you have intent, you have expressions of greatness, and you have every reason to look forward to the future. In this, you can find a way to take the next level of being into consideration to pull you out of your grief and into your next phase.

Your way of spirit *has always been in you*. It has been in you since before you were born.

> *You have Divine gifts that you were born with*
> *that will never see the light of day until you*
> *learn to grieve properly.*

In this, it is all about shedding the beliefs and addressing the fears that have plagued you. So we will summarize what has been said in our previous book[2] to ensure you get this, because it is very important.

Address your beliefs and fears

Your beliefs create your reality. It is not a matter of chanting mantras. It is totally a matter of looking at everything that you think and feel and deciding to address the beliefs that are limiting your joy and passion about life.

The purpose of love is to love self foremost, then to express that love to others, not to use love as something to be bartered, like something that you would share only if you receive it back. Poppycock!

> *Love is all about trusting yourself in the world and*
> *expressing what is deep inside you.*

---

[2] *The Way of Spirit: Teachings of Rose*

You have chosen to forget how very deeply you have been loved into existence because you wanted to have the experience of remembrance, of realizing this. But now is the time to realize it, and in your way of spirit, you have the means to love yourself more.

But the most important of all the practices—including the *Rest in Rose* practice, which we highly suggest is the way to connect deeply with spirit—is to look at each of your beliefs to see what is distressing you. [3] Because every time you have distress, you have beliefs that are not working for you.

Sometimes these beliefs have to do with immortality. If you do not believe you are immortal, that's okay. It is not beneficial all the time to believe this, since the belief keeps you safe from being hit by a car if you don't cross the street properly. Some beliefs are important to keep in place. But with regard to immortality, sometimes you need to just realize that you are, indeed, immortal.

Now, in this idea is also a fear: you fear because you need to take action. When your beliefs make you fear, you need to pay attention to the fear. You acknowledge the fear, then you take action, like stepping out of the way of a car. This is about immortality, too, because you know you don't really die. But in your case, you need to address what you *can* control, and in this, the pressures around

---

[3] See the *Rest in Rose* practice on page 132 and *Identify, Define, and effortlessly Address to your beliefs (IDEA)* practice on page 134.

you have grown so great that you don't know what you can or can't control anymore. So we will help you see the world differently so you can have a clearer view of what you can and can't control.[4]

There is nothing in the world that spiritual practice can't solve, in the sense that you can learn to respond to the world in different ways. You may not always be able to have things in your control, as we said, but you can take on the world in ways that help it. What you can and can't do in this regard is up to you. However, there are significant differences between individuals regarding what they can and can't do, and these are called intents.

Claim your intent

Each individual is born with a unique intent in life.[5] The intent that you were born with has been in design for millions of years, because that's how long it has taken for you to be equipped with the inner senses—as well as intellect—that can do good things in the world. You have lost some of your inner senses in the process, but are beginning to reclaim them.

The sense that you may notice as "spidey tingling" when you know something is not what it seems, for example, has been defeated very much by your belief that you don't have intuition. So you are having to relearn how

---

[4] See *Address and Release Your Fears* practice on page 135.
[5] See the *Find Your Intent* practice on page 136.

to notice and use some of your inner senses all over again. Some instinctive and intuitive senses will be strong in you and some will not. And in this, your intent lies.

When you were born, you knew what your intent was, but it was scared out of you at an early age. How can you survive in the world only relying on your instincts? What would the world be like if you were to only do what you wanted to do?

There are some benefits to this logic, but doing what you *really* want to do is the point. The world needs you to do what you *deeply desire*, not what you *want* to do.

The desires that you have are aligned very closely with your intent in life. Your desires are things like clean air, clean water, love for all creatures, etc., not what society has taught you to want: things.

So in this, realize that the things in your life are fine, just so overrated that you have grown to feel that your life's purpose is to merely achieve the accumulation of wealth. Therefore, you base your self-worth on this point system of valuable things that really may not hold much value for you. In reality, these things do not have much significance when compared to the beautiful world you want, or the things you want to share with it.

This is where your intent comes in, because when you listen to the depths of your soul, you realize that you have a purpose to your life, and to enjoy living that purpose is what the loss, grief, and everyday pains are all about. *They move you into new selfhood.*

When you were little, and you lost that pencil, you had a feeling that there was something in you that was great. You had a feeling that you can take things on in ways you hadn't before. Now, we are not saying that it means getting up out of your chair and cruising about looking for your pencil as much as it does getting out of your seat and saying that you have lost it.

There's a difference between *looking* for something than there is *claiming you have need* for something. The reason we make this distinction is because your intent needs to be *claimed*, and in claiming what is yours the real magic happens. Looking about will only get you so far, as the thing you lost may be hidden or may be taken. However, when you claim something—like the loss of something—you say, "I'm here to experience what's next and I can only do so by saying aloud that I am here to make this right."

How does this apply to the loss of a loved one? Identifying your need is important. You have lost something. You have striven to be the best person you can, and you have had something taken from you in the sense of natural causes or in some evil (which we define as *lacking compassion*) way.

So in your desire to stand up for what was lost, you say, "I'm ready to take this on now."

Now, we will also say that in your charged view of grief, you sometimes miss the obvious: pain has as much power as love, because it is a form of love that is never satisfied.

Pain helps you realize what's in need of your immediate attention. When you are in pain, your every mood is based on this pain.

However, pain can be avoided by doing what? Loving self. We'll explain.

In standing up for yourself, you gain the freedom to say, "I don't want to do this anymore. I need something or somebody to stand up for me and help me into the next phase where I can gain what I really lost."

We say *really* lost because what you *have* lost is important, not what it *seems you have* lost—the loved one—who, in spite of how you may think, has reason to move on. He or she has needed to go to where they can sort out the next phase for themselves. If you have lost someone, it is through your recognition they live in you that is important.

So your belief in the afterlife is needed to help you through this. Even if you don't believe in the afterlife, taking the time to consider that your loved one is out of pain now is helpful. However, as we said, this is not always accurate, nor is it always helpful when considering your own immortality.

In this, the reasons for saying "I need help" are to allow yourself to realize that:

1) you are not alone in this world,

2) you have spiritual beings around to help you, and

3) you are willing to change

Access alternative actions

So, back to your pencil proclamation: what are you proclaiming? "I have made myself aware that I have lost something that's important to me. I would appreciate some help in getting this situation resolved."

The pencil is now part of a greater scenario that you have needed to move into so you can consider the new self that you *will be* when you get through it. The self that you *are* needs to take flight in new ways. However, you can't do it without help.

The real question is: how can you move into new areas of expression *now* in ways that will be most fulfilling?

You may need to beat up somebody to get your pencil back. This is not an aggressive action that we would typically condone, but it speaks to what you sometimes think of as new areas of expression, and taking on bullies is an important thing. Perhaps you may consider how the bully would feel. These are all ways to access alternatives to see which would be the most fulfilling, and basically any idea during this phase is acceptable, not to say it would be acceptable to act on it.

So in sorting out ideas that will move you into new areas of expression, think about everything. Think about taking off from school to go home and tell your mother you love her. These are all ways to express yourself despite how you think you *should* express yourself. You might even take up a collection to get what you have lost back into your life again.

Do you see how this would take hold in ways that may suit you very well? In this, your intent will guide you into the places you most likely—and most happily—will go, because your intent is all about your expressions.

Say you are a child of two who has prematurely lost a tooth. What does this do for the child? Causes them pain, perhaps, or causes them some grief when the parent has found out and does not like it. But when you consider that the fear is what's in need of losing, you can get a sense about grief. The child will cry, perhaps, and even scream at the fear, but the child will quite naturally then go on with their life. It will learn to lose the fear as well, when it realizes that mother really does get wound too tight about these things.

Your inner senses know these things. That's why we are so very persistent in acknowledging intent, because it has everything to do with your intuition.

Now, perhaps you want to throttle somebody who has taken something away from you. Perhaps that's something you need to consider—however, no intent involves throttling somebody without very good reason. Look at the many wars that you create because you think you've lost something that somebody has taken, when in reality you perhaps needed to lose it.

Do you care about whether you throttle somebody or not? Yes you do. In fact, this is potentially the worst thing you can do. Can you stand up to bullies and tell them, "Hey, I think you may have my pencil. I'd like it back"? Yes, you can. In fact, this is what grief does: it moves you into new areas of expression, sometimes in ways you've never considered. If you have not taken on a bully, maybe you need to.

Do you see what loss then does to move you into spaces of greater self-love? Do you understand that when you grieve, you set forth new allowances for everything in your world? When you take on a bully, do you see how that one act can ripple throughout the world in ways that cause more bullies to be stood up to?

Only your actions can improve your life.

So taking on bullies, taking on whoever has caused your loss, can be a good thing for you and for the world.

In this, you have a sense there are options that have not been discovered yet. What if the boy or girl with the lost pencil were to suddenly see that the pencil needed losing? Perhaps it was an old pencil the dog chewed on and it really didn't need to be in use anymore, except it was the only one the boy or girl had. Then claiming the loss would be even more beneficial, would it not? Wouldn't claiming the loss to potentially get a better pencil be an action that you would want to take?

We are not suggesting that you have reason to want to have a better person replace your friend or loved one who has passed, but it's important to consider that maybe the person needed to be removed from your life so you could make it different and better. It's not to say that they were in any way causing you harm. It's that they may have been too dependent upon you, or you on them, and you needed to depend on yourself more.

There are infinite reasons for loss. These are only a few. But they point out that there is every reason to begin to redefine yourself in terms of your loss. And claiming it is important.

Address your pain

Now, grief is also a gift. It helps you realize how painful life can be. We do not mean to say pain is *good*, but it is *necessary*. Pain is your own expression of depth, and you can't know life well without it. The pain you feel, though, is for your purposes of looking at what needs to be looked at. Pain has many purposes, but above all, this is what is in play when you grieve.

The purpose of pain, too, is to allow as well as remove it. There's no cause worth having pain about, period. There's no suffering that is good or holy. We want you to remove your beliefs about good and bad pain, for pain is there for your noticing only, not to hold onto. If you are holding onto your pain because you think it is sacred, *don't*. This is another belief to address.

> *Pain is to be addressed, and is never*
> *something to hang onto.*

Now, sometimes people do hold onto pain as well as suffering. Why? Because they haven't claimed their suffering or loss. They have not extended into the world enough to know what the next steps are, partially because they have tried to do the necessary grief work alone.

But there's an expiration date on grief, and this is needed when you have thoughts that your grief needs to go on until you die.

That's not your *will* talking—that's your *culture* talking—because people really don't want to do that. They have been taught that grieving is somewhat of a sacred thing to do on an ongoing basis. But fear and grief will only *erode* your sacred space, not *enhance* it. Here's why.

Give yourself space

The space that you give yourself to grieve is perhaps the most important thing you can do. The space is necessary, whether it is a space of joy with others surrounding you, or a space of deep regret and pain while you work out what you need to, addressing what you could have done better, if anything.

> *The space to grieve is the best thing you*
> *can give yourself should you*
> *encounter severe loss.*

The many small opportunities for grief need only to be processed, then recovered from quickly, as in the case of the lost pencil. When your fears go too deep, the space needs to be created and protected. This is symbolic of the journey inward, but is not necessarily something you do alone or for a long time.

You have ideas that grief is some extended funeral mood in which you have every reason to feel terrible, but it's not. Grief is often a joyous experience when you realize its gifts.

As we said, the purpose to grief is to give you the time and space to complete the process of letting go of what you need to let go of.

The reason to let go of things is so you can —
as a soul having human experiences —
learn what it's like to be a human
having spiritual experiences.

The reason we are saying this twice, in effect, is so you really can grasp the truth of the sentence: that life is all about spiritual development that exists in concert with your human development, too. The process can be long or short, tall or wide, but the essence is always the same: to let go of what you need to let go of.

What do you need to let go of? Everything that makes you miserable. Realize you are not letting go of an aunt or uncle, mother or father. In reality, you are letting go of whatever holds you from being happy.

In this, *the thing has always existed to be let go of, you just haven't realized it before.*

LET THAT SHIT GO

Find the fear under denial and anger

Take, for example, if you have done something to harm somebody who has not yet realized it. Say this person dies. What do you feel? You feel shame, perhaps, or you feel that you can do better, or that you would not do this again to somebody.

Has the thing interrupted your sleep in the meantime? Maybe it has and maybe it hasn't. Does it come to the surface of your consciousness while you are grieving? Yes it does. What does it do to get your attention? That's the important part.

What it may do—not always—is to force itself into your awareness through anger or denial. Denial is harder to notice, but anger, you know, is easy.

Take, for example, a person who has something to face, like a past episode of humiliating someone who has now passed, and somebody else who has not any reason to feel badly about this situation. The first one can either deny or express anger or remorse, if they notice that they have feelings about the situation. The denial comes through in ways that would be least obvious, such as through an editorial about the person, spoken or not spoken, in which they claim to always have treated this person wonderfully well.

Anybody in that situation who thinks about their actions as only wonderful denies themselves the inner knowledge that is required for healing.

Anger will come out in any number of ways, as you can guess, because there are often fights started with other mourners, for example. There might be two individuals who need to express their own remorse at their actions, who express any number of variations of denial and anger.

In every case, fear is at the bottom of the response.

Fear is what makes people respond in ways that ultimately can be thought of as healthy when the fear is addressed. Anger and denial are merely responses of fear that they did not do well enough. The fear is purposeful, as fear always is, in our estimation.

Fear is a wonderful friend because it helps you recognize where there's a problem, so you may address the problem.

Fear helps animals, for example, to realize they need to move to another living spot because they sense there is a predator nearby who has just moved into the neighborhood. So fear is good when it provokes you to look for options to address a problem. In this, the *accessing of alternatives* response described earlier is the best way to do so.

The capable person will find ways to address the problem by suggesting to himself that he can do better, period. They will also summon up the courage to admit that they have been wrong in the past. Some will want to make restitution to somebody. However, the main thing is to realize the problem and own up to it. This involves owning up to self only, not necessarily to do anything to compensate.

The point is that you must—every chance you get—realize you *will* make mistakes, allow yourself to let go of what you *can't* control, then take what you *can* control and make the best of it.

Chapter 4:
Receive the Gifts

When we last left our hero with the pencil that had disappeared, he was telling the class about his issue. He professed—indeed claimed—that he had lost his pencil. In this, he expressed a need to find it.

The reason we say this again is that you also must realize that you need to express to somebody, including yourself, what you have done "wrong". In this case, he did nothing wrong, he just has a problem.

Yet remember, he is not the sort of person who can admit that some things are out of his control, and attaches to the pencil things that may not be true. He thinks his lack of whatever—focus or determination—has prevented him from holding on to his pencil. So already he has something to let go of.

In professing that he has lost his pencil, he is letting go of a lot of stuff he needs to let go of: fear that he is not perfect, fear that he will antagonize somebody who's stolen his pencil, fear that the teacher will not like him for saying something during class.

This is perhaps the most important part of the grief process: to admit that you have lost something. This has everything to do with how you proceed down the path toward healing.

Now, what about this seems so big to us spirits and not to you, perhaps? It's that *you have not been taught to lose.*

You have been taught to only win, and this is perhaps the root of the problem that many people have with letting things go. Because you often say to yourself, "I don't think I really need to see this as a loss," you deflect any growth opportunity that you have to push you into your next path of happiness. Because grief is exactly that.

> *Grief is the means to push you into*
> *your next path of happiness.*

Fearlessness

To summon the fearlessness of loss is the most important thing you might do. We suggest you lose something every day—your pocketbook, your fears about something, your internalizing of what you need to express—all these are things to lose to put you on your next path to happiness. Each one says to you that the purpose of your life is not to always hold onto things, and that you need to sometimes let go.

Take, for example, how you may respond to losing your pocketbook or wallet. It is perhaps the most valuable object in your possession.

How would you respond? With fear, of course.

What about the fear would be helpful? It would make you realize you need to be more careful with valuable things.

What about this is beneficial? Perhaps there are other areas of your life that require more focus because they are important.

What do you do when you have fear visit you and tell you to be more careful with valuable things? You take action. You take greater care of your valuables, or you deny there's a problem, which happens more than you think it does.

Anger certainly is invoked when something like this happens, but these are all fear-based scenarios that help you realize you must act on something you have lost.

Other things are lost that do not require much attention: skin cells, dead things that live in your system, lightbulbs that burn out, ephemeral things that do not require much attention.

Do you mourn these? We say, yes you do, because when you mourn them, you see these things as fragile parts of life that escape your noticing, perhaps, but are part of the reason you chose to be alive. These things equip you with what you need to live your best life. What better way to honor them than to say, "I love you and mourn the fact that you are gone, but I look forward to future times with new body cells and light bulbs"?

*What better way to honor your world than to
send it a message that you love it dearly?*

Knowing the world is here to serve you

We will say this is not necessarily what you want to do every time you lose a skin cell. The point is that you must realize that the world is here to serve you.

The world is here to serve you in the best ways *it knows how,* not in the ways *you think it should.* Some things will die—and must die—in order to make room for new things. It knows better than you what needs to die and what doesn't need to die.

In this, the real value of mourning occurs because you have a sense the world has reason to show you things that you would not normally ask for.

*The world knows better than
you what you need.*

This is something of an odd statement—isn't it?—because you've been taught that you are to sublimate Nature and everything around you. But Nature—as we will say in other words as *spiritual life*—will always know what's best for you. You see this when you really look.

How many times have you not gotten what you thought you wanted, only to get something better than you expected? How many times have you been let down, only to find there was purpose to that, or reason for it to get you into a space where you could fully thrive?

The best self is merely the person you are becoming. The world helps you to do that.

Letting go of guilt

When we last left our hero, he had recognized that it was okay to claim his loss. He knew he wasn't going to benefit from denying or being angry about his loss. He realized that he was not to blame for it.

But what if he had been to blame for his loss? What if he had done something that made this loss permanent, such as threw it at somebody who had confiscated it? In other words, he was totally to blame for the loss.

What then?

If he had really thought about it, he would have realized he was to blame. Otherwise, if he hadn't really thought of it, he would set himself into the anger and denial part of the grief process.

But in this case, let's say he didn't consider that he was responsible, even though he was. He says that he has lost his pencil. The world, perhaps through the words or facial expression of a fellow student, says to him, "You threw it at somebody. Therefore, you're to blame for it."

Then what happens? He realizes he's the one who needed to adjust his actions *before* his actions took place. Now he has lost his precious pencil.

What about this has to do with death of a family member? Nothing, if you have no reason to fear that you have done something to make the loss happen. Everything, if you feel guilty for the loss.

This is the hardest part about the grief process: admitting that you have done something to contribute to the loss.

Contributing to the loss of a loved one sounds like a pretty open and shut case. Did you create the accident or the illness they died from? If not, then you have nothing to fear, right? Wrong.

There are many reasons to consider that you had something to do with the loss of a loved one. In fact, you do this more than you think you do. You say, "I could have been kinder. I could have gone to their place more often." Perhaps you had reason to see them and you didn't, perhaps even to prolong their life with kind words or gestures.

Did you have something to do with their death? Yes, because you just assumed you did. Now, this assumption may be correct or incorrect.

The point is, do you think you had something to do with it? This is an important question. If you do, then you need to look deeply at how you go about your days and see if there's something you need to change.

Recognizing natural guilt vs. artificial guilt

Most individuals have some sort of guilt about the passing of a loved one. This might include things they have done that are violations, such as not taking care of someone well enough or being unkind in ways that are not appropriate.

Being unkind in itself *is not* wrong, but being unkind in ways that are violations *is* wrong. If you have reason to address your lack of kindness or care, you need to say, "I will do better next time." You summon up the courage to admit you were wrong.

> *This is the most important part of the grief process: realizing what you could do better.*

Now, if you have reason to believe that your guilt is not well-founded, this is another step towards getting over the loss in positive ways. If you believe that what you did was not any reason to feel guilty, you need to let the guilt go.

For example, if you have had a fight with your sister, and she called you a bad word, and you called her that word back, maybe you needed to do that, and it wasn't a real reason to feel guilty. Maybe it was.

Do you feel guilty? Maybe you do and maybe you don't. The point is, how do you feel inside?

This takes time to wade through, but is purposeful in its reasons for being in your thoughts. Could you have done better? Maybe.

If you have done something to make someone angry, this is not always bad. Sometimes people are just going to be angry. The point is, what have you done to them, really? And in this, there's a gem that we will share now.

Everybody—each person who has ever lived—
creates their own reality.

This is not to say you don't create the reality you share together. This is known as co-creation. However, everyone has choices as well as paths to follow. You can't make anybody angry, in a sense. They *choose* to respond with anger.

Perhaps you have provoked them intentionally. This is not always wrong either. The point is, what does your intuition tell you? Is it wrong to provoke someone or not?

In every case, you need to look at this with your moral intuition and see how this feels. Was it a violation or not?

Do you see how very important this exercise is in promoting your own sense of well-being? Do you see how sorting out *natural guilt—what you know deep down to be a response to violation—*is key to letting go of your grief and fear?

Natural guilt is a response from the primitive ways that you knew as animal selves, who knew deep down that every life is precious. You have this same response in you, but you tend to realize thoughts and rationale to express that this is not correct. But it *is* correct. You use your instincts to sort out what is real, what is false, and what is or isn't a violation the same way animals do. You know before you take any action if the action will violate.

So when you mourn, you get a sense of how animals mourn, too. You sense that the purpose for this loss is good, but it's hard, because now you need to go forward without it. The sense about animals is important.

You need to ensure that your life is inherently good, and there's no better choice of role model than animals.

Now, in this sorting out of good guilt vs. bad guilt, realize that bad guilt—*artificial guilt*—needs to be addressed in every way. You have been taught to toe the line: not speak up, always say your prayers, relate to others with niceness, and let others have their say while you don't. This is sometimes true and sometimes not true.

The point is: what do you really believe? If you have reason to believe that you have dignity, purpose, and love, you have reasons to express this. You do not need to borrow someone else's pencil if you don't have reason to do so. It's important that you have *your* pencil, *your* means for expression in the world.

The pencil isn't just a metaphor for something that is lost: *the pencil represents your expressions and your reason for living.*

Now let's get back to your expressions of claiming that you lost your pencil. "Dammit! I lost my pencil!" might work, or, "Has anybody seen my pencil?" But what will not work is, "I can't find my pencil and I will just sit here with the loss unexpressed and go about my business mourning the loss."

This is not healthy, yet *this is what people do all the time.*

And in this, the sense of loss does nothing to help anybody. It just shuts down expressions of feeling and the ability to address one's fears, guilt, and other emotions that come up during the course of grieving.

New ways to express yourself

The pencil is also a metaphor for how one works their magic in the world. The thing to realize about pencils is you can use them in a multitude of ways. You can write, draw, throw them, take out an eyeball if you're not careful, and other things.

Expressions, therefore, have purpose. They have meaning.

This is how you can think about having purpose: having a pencil in your hand, ready to do business and artistry. For in your expressions of loving intention in the world, your pencils *rule!*

Now, it stands to reason that if you were to get past the emotions of anger, guilt, fear, and regret, you would sense something else coming up in you. You would sense that the reasons for guilt are good. You *can* do better next time, perhaps. You *must* do better is an even better response, because it summons in you your heroic self.

This is a big topic so let us summarize what we have taught you in this chapter.

- **The bridge to getting through emotion is to recognize what is going on inside you.** Fear will be the first response: what do you need to do to address the situation? Then do it.

- **If you have guilt or anger, you need to address the reasons for it.** This is the hardest part about grief work, because facing how you are in the world is the most stressful thing you might do. The denial of the problem is worse, because you will not find out what the rewards of your grief will be. You will shut down everything that is special about you and how you will move forward with your new creative expressions.

- **The rewards of grief are great**, as long as you do the work required to get through it.

Chapter 5: Realize
Your Heroic Journey

The path for you is in getting the best self in charge, then working towards realizing your greater purpose. We call these the *heroic self* and the *heroic journey*. They are part of the reason you have chosen to be alive.

The other reasons are about realizing that you are only human. The human self constantly needs to be attended while you do your great things in the world.

This is the purpose of grief: to show you who you are and who you need to be next.

The reason we call this the heroic self and the heroic journey is that everything around you points you to your heroic self and heroic journey.

In fact, the purpose for life is to help you on your way.

Is that magnificent or what? Imagine that everything around you conspires for your happiness. How wonderful it is to be so loved!

Despite how you feel about yourself—you sometimes even think you're bad—realize you're just a human being having an emotional crisis while your heroic self works out the details of how you will want to be different next time.

This is part of the lesson of grief: it helps you connect with the heroic self you want to be next.

Now, this is sometimes tricky to realize, for you have not thought about yourself as a heroic being before, perhaps. But you are, and every stone, twig, and bird feather around you knows this, although your ego says, "Wait a minute. I'm not comfortable with that. I'm going to sit here with my pencil less hand and continue to wait for something good to happen to me."

But things that are wrong or bad will always happen. In fact, this is part of the reason you chose this life, so you could surmount those things.

Follow your passions

Now, when you are distressed, and when you are fearful, are when you are the most beautiful, in some ways, because you recognize the need to assert something deep within you that has gone unexpressed.

If you are fearful, you need to know what actions to take.

If you are in denial, you need to wake up to the fact that you caused some harm and examine this.

If you have reason to feel badly, you need to make amends if necessary, then follow your passions into the next phase. Because here's the key:

It is the result of not following your passions that has gotten you into this predicament in the first place.

So you have summoned all your courage and decided to look inside yourself to see what you could do better, if anything. Perhaps you decided that you can be better at being kind to others.

This is a very good thing, if you are correct about this, because kindness only goes so far. Sometimes you put aside your own expressions to be kind to others.

This may be something to look at, and in this, "What are you being so subservient for?" might be a question that arises. For if you have put aside your passions to instill in everybody the fact that you are the kindest person they know, they may not appreciate it, nor is it necessarily your path of happiness, which we define as your way of spirit.

This has to do with getting what you *want* rather than what you *need* and *desire*, and the desire deep within you is always about your passions and making sure you follow them.

So if you are holding onto something that you need to let go of, chances are you need to focus on what really satisfies you, and look at how this loss has been helpful in realizing this.

The path for you is different after grieving than it is before grieving.

The difference will correspond with the *degree* in which you effectively grieve—not the *length*—for continuing to grieve after the grief period should have ended is why you have depression. We will say more about depression a little later, but for now, you can think of depression as *what occurs when you continue to grieve after grief's expiration date.*

The path for you is lengthy. It goes on forever. We're talking, of course, about your eternal essence Self—the Self you really are when you're not thinking about yourself as ego. The path is lengthy, wide, variety-filled, and fun... yes, *fun!* There's not any reason to ever feel that death is anything but passage into the next phase.

This is another belief that you need to address. Death is never final. So if you are holding on to archaic beliefs about this being the end, you are incorrect.

Let go of your fears

When the world tells you to let go, you need to let go. When your heart tells you that you can do better and have more fun through following your passions, you need to believe it. The heart and mind need to be totally in synch during this process.

What better way than to let go of whoever you thought you were than to embrace your new self? In this, the new self you embrace is the new heroic self that you have needed to become.

Now, there is often reluctance to embrace this self because of many reasons: fear of disappointing others, fear of losing something else in the process, fear of not having what you had before the changes you went through. These are all reasons to fear. And in this, the fears can be addressed.

What do you really think about the people who think you will let them down? Is it artificial guilt? Is it a solid reputation that you risk? Do you care too much about what others think about you?

This is a very different sort of grieving now, isn't it? This is all about moving into a new self without anybody's permission except your own.

So, for example, after a loved one has died, did you feel you needed to move into new areas of expression? Or perhaps you had lost a job that brought you much satisfaction.

What is the world trying to tell you? To move on.

What will you do to engage—in new way—the purpose that you were born with? Whatever you feel inside is what needs to be done.

So you grieve, you let go of what you need to let go of, then you say, "What now? What can I do to really make myself happy?" Because, as we said, you may not be doing so, and the grieving process is showing you that.

Learn from others

When you hear about the death of a famous, beloved person by suicide, you say to yourself "How can that be? How can they be gone now?"

Perhaps that person has struggled with depression. The reason for this is they have not made the transition into their next phase. They are grieving something that has reduced their capability to respond to life in ways that bring them joy again. They may have obligations they feel they cannot overcome. They may feel that life is getting old. They may look at suicide as a means to escape. The many reasons for this have to do with grieving.

The best thing you can do to grieve the loss of these brilliant individuals is to say, "What have I learned from this?" Isn't this exactly what you have wanted to hear about your grief in losing them, so you can let go of the things they needed to, the many reasons that they were depressed—that they have shared with you—so you can live more fully and with more passion and happiness?

Do you sense that if they'd determined that grieving has benefits, and they could work through their grief with the help of a counselor, they'd have found peace and happiness in their lives?

Some individuals take medications that can impair the ability to resolve their grief by adding a clouding layer of sedation. Sedation is not a bad thing, it's something required to help individuals realize they are safe and taken care of.

However, when sedation imparts to the individual the message that sedation is the key to getting by, that's where the problem starts. Sedation is only a short-term medicine to help people through trauma. The drugs have little usefulness when extended beyond the natural point where the individual needs to take hold of their new self.

Trust in your heroic self

Why is this so different, this idea of taking hold of your new self? Because of how you may think of yourselves as heroic.

The path for you has been difficult at times, even at early ages, perhaps.

The path has also been tested repeatedly for you,
and you have realized many things about love and
life that seem very permanent, but aren't, because
they are what you needed then, not now.

The heroic self that you know as you, therefore, is shaped by your past. The past has shaped you into a person who has surmounted much in order to achieve the life you know now. The struggle to continue this sometimes seems too much for people.

The way to get over this is to realize that your heroic self will always pull you out of whatever slump you're in.

This is another wonderful thing about grieving: the heroic self knows what you need.

Now let's go back to the boy with the pencil. The pencil wants to be found. The pencil is the person's intent in life, the reason for being in the world. There's no better friend than the pencil, as it represents everything that this person will do with his life, as he knows this is all about his expressions.

Your expressions are needed in the world. There is no substitute for you. You hold the keys to many peoples' fortunes as loving individuals by the expressions of love that you create in the world.

We need to say, too, that the intent, or purpose, of your life is not what you may think. Your purpose is to express yourself *in spite* of the many challenges you have and also *because* of them. Your pain, denying of self, everything that you are, goes into your life's purpose.

Your intent has to do with how you express your life through the many forms that it may take.

Your intent, therefore, is very important because *it is how you move that pencil every day that needs satisfaction.*

LET THAT SHIT GO

Let pain tell you what you need

The purpose for your life, therefore, incorporates pain as well as freedom to express yourself.

Incorporating pain does not make you less of an individual. In fact, pain has to be in your world for many reasons, not only to force you to make changes to stop it— because that's its predominant function—but also to express in the world what you feel deep down is the right thing for you and for the world.

Therefore,

In finding your own means to stop your pain,
you find ways to stop the pain of others.

The purpose of pain is to end it. The purpose of pain is to recognize in yourself what really needs to change. What your path reveals to you isn't always perfection. Pain, though, is not antithetical to perfection, it's a means to recognize how you must go forward without such grand ideas about it.

The purpose, therefore, of pain is to let go of what
you need to in order to be fully human.

There's a vast difference between what you *think* you need in life and what you *really do* need in life. The pain helps you get past the things you *think* you need so as to incorporate what you really *do* need. Sometimes what you need is to lose things.

We'll go back to our friend looking for his pencil to evoke in you the suffering that goes along with this sort of action.

The pain that our friend has is starting to reveal itself. He's sweating from nerves as he's thinking the teacher may not like his disruption of the class. He is putting himself out there for everybody to see he has lost something. Some people may think he's a loser.

How is this different than losing a loved one? It's not because you have beliefs that losing somebody makes you "a loser", per se. It points out that you have not enough "whatever it takes to live the most perfect life and, therefore, never losing anything."

This is more evident in the sense of losing in the stock market, capital gains, or what have you. The point is that you need to let go of your beliefs that loss is bad. The loss you need is always going to find you.

Loss is needed for you to grow.

Now, what does our friend do if he is a good boy? He apologizes.

Do you think this is what the world needs, to apologize for what you have lost? Not at all. The boy feels badly for disrupting the class, perhaps, but to be apologetic for loss is something else to look at.

There's no need to feel badly for any reason that you lose, not even if it occurs to you that it might be disruptive to others. This is another way you think loss is bad.

If he goes from chair to chair looking for his pencil, it's all good. Why? Because everyone in the class needs to support him in his loss. It takes time to sort out what's needed and what isn't. If the loss requires somebody to say, "I need *this* now" or "I need *that* now from you," then that's something to do.

What if somebody has mistakenly taken his pencil or has taken it to purposefully steal it? The world needs to pay attention to the loss and support the person in their time of letting go while trying to capture what it is that is *truly* lost. We'll explain.

Reach out to others to find what you really lost

When you grieve, you have more reason to reach out to others to reframe what it is that you really lost.

Perhaps if you have lost a loved one to cancer, you feel as though you have lost not only the person—because that's a huge loss for you in itself—but also, you've lost faith in your medical establishment, or in the food you eat, or any number of things that go along with the loss.

What better way to find what you need than to work this out with counselors, therapists, or other sorts of people who will bring you guidance with regard to gaining in the process?

For example, perhaps there's reason to look at the water that you drink to see if it's healthy. This goes back to the idea that in producing fears, you have the opportunity to address them. You look at things differently when you address what you can and can't control.

What better way to address something that you feel deeply must change? You would perhaps launch a drive to get better water into your taps, or to promote greater health awareness for cancer. These are all beautiful expressions that you would find by sorting out what you do and do not require in life.

The pencil, therefore, isn't just a way to get closer to others in your time of grief. It's a way to enjoy the best of what is available to you, to get closer to what it is you really desire from life.

The point is that the purpose of loss is not to distract you from your ideas of shiny perfection, nor is it to punish you or make you feel badly having lost something.

The point of loss is to get you
moving in new directions.
That's all this is about.

So when you lose something, you antagonize yourself, perhaps, for a while, you get angry with yourself or others. Perhaps you don't realize it, but you shut down in some ways. Then you say, "I can do this better. I can let go of what I don't really need and get past the point of needing to compensate for the loss. I can express myself differently."

The purpose, therefore, is to *get past compensatory actions* that stuff down your fears or fill you with unworthy things—for example, to eat, drink, or take drugs to suppress your hurt or feelings of emptiness. Only then can you become more yourself.

> *The path for you is laid bare with grief,*
> *and this is a good thing.*

Address beliefs that run counter to your healing

Sometimes you don't find the path right away because you have beliefs that run counter to your healing. We will give you a list of them here, because they are important to recognize so you can navigate through any loss—from loss of a loved one to loss of something that seems insignificant but may not be when you really look at it.

- **Take into consideration that the path for you is not supposed to be perfect or without loss.** Take heart that loss is a necessary and beautiful thing, as much as you may think gain is.

- **Align your beliefs in ways that support loss, not fight it.** The loss is purposeful, as is everything in your life. The path for you is to go without this thing or person, not with it.

- **Realize that some things can be replaced by common-sense solutions.** However, not everything can. Try to find the purpose for the loss before you replace it. There's purpose to everything, even noticing something that you may not have realized was important.

- **Try to bring in people who will support you in your journey through the grief.** Extra care needs to be taken with this part. The people you need are those who believe in death as a passage into the next phase, and believe that things in life need time to heal, for example. You will know the right person or persons when you find them.

- **Take care to let go of what you need to without feeling the need to be in control of everything.** The path is always about turning over what you can't control to God, Essence, Divine, Spirit, whatever you call it.

- **The path is always greater when you create your reality in ways that are sustainable.** Look to your beliefs to support who you need to be next. If the person you are does not work for you anymore, let go of what you need to so you can get past the grief and recreate your reality in ways that suit you.

Chapter 6: Find the Better Alternatives

Now, when we last left our hero, he was struggling with the fact that he had disrupted the class with his many questions about life—and the pursuit of whatever it is that you pursue as humans—and he began asking questions that matter.

He started asking others, "What is it that I really want to accomplish with this pencil anyway? Does this really need to be something I have in my book bag, or is it not needed?"

If you don't need it, let it go. If you think you need it, then look at why you need it: to express yourself.

Can you get by without it? Maybe yes, maybe no.

Is there a better alternative to all these questions? Not really. However, there will be alternatives that present themselves when you get past the pain of loss.

We'll explain.

FIND THE BETTER ALTERNATIVES

Beautiful things will present themselves

The path of grief always yields new, beautiful things. We'll repeat that.

> *The path of grief always yields*
> *new, beautiful things.*

Now, you may find that you don't like what you lost and replace it with something better.

Or you may find that you make friends along the way, looking for what you think you need.

Or you find out that the world is friendlier than you thought, that your teacher really does care about you, and that the pencil has been found in ways that are funny, perhaps in the nose of somebody you think likes you and wants to make you laugh.

Do you see how this might turn out if you really didn't need the pencil, too? How might this work? Perhaps you found a better pencil in your book bag that you needed all along because it was special, or automatic, or any number of things that occurred to you during the process of letting go of your fears around the pencil.

> *Because that's what grief is ultimately*
> *about: losing the fears you have about*
> *whatever it is that comes up from*
> *the process itself.*

You can be happy all the time

Now, despite what you have found about loss in the past, the best way to consider loss is as a friend who tells you something you need to know.

The path for you is fraught with all sorts of messages about how to live, how to do things, and how to be a better person. Many of these aren't helpful, especially if "being a better person" means beating yourself up for who you have been. To clarify our meaning of the expression,

You may need to be a better person, but more importantly, you need to be a happy person all the time.

We know this sounds terrible to somebody who is grieving. Be happy all the time? Yet this is the essence of grief, too, because when you take on the process, you will feel lighter and more capable of joy than you ever believed possible. The reason for this is because you will allow yourself to be truly human.

This takes getting used to, because you have been taught that you need to suffer, but the reality is that while suffering is an important part of life, you don't need to suffer to be human. You need to be human to suffer. There's a difference.

Suffering has merits in that it tells you that you're human. If you see someone suffering, you feel badly, and want to assist them. This is because you are Divine. You are Divine because you're human.

FIND THE BETTER ALTERNATIVES

There's not any difference between being
fully human and being Divine.

So if you feel the world has caused you suffering, embrace that, because that's exactly why you chose to be here: to learn to suffer in ways that are healthy, not unhealthy.

In your course of action is the key to how to control what you *can* control and let go of what you *can't*.

You can let go of what you can't control

When you let go of what you can't control, you sense the world is going to be alright because it's in good hands: the hands of Goodness, Godness, Essence, Divinity, whatever you call it.

The world is what it is supposed to be all the time, and will be okay without your feeling you have to suffer too much.

In your development is the key to relieving yourself of the burden of feeling responsible for every hurt that occurs in the world. You need to let go of what you can't control. In this,

You can control things that will lessen
suffering for yourself as well as others.
The way to do so is to let go of your suffering
so you can help others let go of theirs.

This requires a broader view of what you are than what you have been led to believe.

The world will help you feel better about everything when you discard your notions that you're supposed to be in control of everything.

The world is here to support you always. This is perhaps the biggest problem with modernity, because you have been taught to be at odds in the world, with everything around you, even Nature itself, even those you love.

When you consider how you feel you need to compete for a person's love, for example, you get the idea that even your own siblings may be competitors. However, this is never the case. You're never supposed to feel that you're in competition.

The world provides enough for everybody, so much so that you create enough abundance in your life to support whatever you need from life.

You create your reality

No one else can be responsible for you because you have complete control of your reality that you create, along with your Personal God. So when you yell, rebel, etc., you are acting in ways that support your growth, but this may not be required since nobody else is responsible for you like you are.

We're not saying parents don't need to nurture children, or that you don't need to take care of others. We're saying that anything that comes your way is a creation of what you have decided to incorporate in your lifetime, thanks to your loving Personal God.

So when you feel like a victim of life, realize you have every reason to get past this belief and get closer to where you need to be in order to be happy again.

With regard to grief, realize that you don't need to suffer with the belief that life is not going to support you. It will always support you, just not always the way you think. In fact, the medications that incorporate focus on thinking do not help you. What helps you is to let go of whatever it is that does not serve you. In this, you need to separate your wants from your desires.

Your desires want you to find them. This is such an important point that we will say this again:

> *Your desires want you*
> *to find them.*

This is so very important that the next section will spur you towards growth more than anything that you might ever read again. Because in your quest for your wants, losses happen, and when they do, your Personal God provides the means to find out what you *truly* want, which is what we call desires.

You can have what you desire

The best way to consider desires are those things that you really want but are too afraid to find. So you content yourself with the wants you have been taught to have instead, such as personal credit lines that allow you to buy what you like, letting others have the last say because you have beliefs about always having to be nice, and being responsible for other peoples' realities.

Each of these has reason to be wanted, because they are not inherently bad or wrong. What's wrong is when you replace what you truly desire with these sorts of wants in ways that distract you from fully living your life.

> *Desires are not only primary to your experiences as designed by your soul — in the sense of what you came here to do and express — they are what everything around you urges you towards so as to get past your grief about what you don't have, to wake up and be happy in the world.*

Desires are so very important to your lives that you think they are bad because that's what you've been taught to avoid: desires.

FIND THE BETTER ALTERNATIVES

Has your religious upbringing disallowed you from even considering your desires? Very much.

So despite what you think about desires, realize that, in our view, the definition is primary to your very existence.

Desires are what you came here to explore,
and anything less is not only unhealthy for you,
it is also potentially fatal.

The purpose of desires is to wean you of what you need to let go of in order to live a full, beautiful life. In this, you can see the connection between loss and gain. If you have lost something, you have lost it for a very good reason, because the path to discovery about the issue at hand is the reason you have created the loss in the first place.

There are very few things that are more important than loss in this regard. It's something that occurs every day, and you don't even think about it when you go to sleep at night. But every loss is a gain.

Here's why. The loss you feel at the end of the day can be used as a means to put more focus on your desires. Take, for example, an episode in your day that causes you some degree of pain because you wish it had gone better.

What do you do? You examine the situation. You see what you could have done better in order to be happier. You let go of what you can't control, and you change what you can. It's very simple. Then you move into the dream state with the sense of urgency about one particular thing or another.

The dream state helps you sort things out, then you wake with new information about what you truly desire. If you have a dream practice—which we highly recommend—you write down what the dream was about, then tune into your Personal God for answers about what you think are the gaps in your understanding.[6]

> *You will always get answers.*
> *You will always get support.*
> *You only need to incorporate the dream*
> *space more into your life than you do now.*

More lessons from celebrities

Take, for example, an actor who has gotten past the point of really enjoying his work. Let's say he's famous and has trouble being in the world now. He is always recognized. He is always asked to pose for photos. He does not enjoy the promise of the next acting job. He has too many relationships with people who only want him for what they can get from him. He goes to sleep every night dreading the next day. Soon he is found dead of an overdose. Sound familiar?

---

[6] See the *Dream Practice* on page 141.

FIND THE BETTER ALTERNATIVES

*These individuals want you to know
what to do differently.*

What better way to explain why you created *their* experiences in *your* reality than to mourn them and learn from them, too?

If you had been the actor, what would you have done? Nothing differently, perhaps, or maybe you would have used this method to realize different options than before.

The path for individuals who are in the public eye speaks of the sorts of pressure that you don't realize in your everyday life. These individuals must often make the sorts of compromises that weigh heavily on them. They are expected to be perfect. They live in others' imaginations as people who don't really do much more than act, for example, or they have many followers on Twitter, or they have many persons attending to them in ways that are artificial. This is something that you may not understand, or perhaps you do.

The purpose for their lives has reached the point of stagnation because there are too many people who trust them completely with their happiness. They begin to feel they will let others down if they don't do some things that they don't feel are right.

This is the problem — *they begin to live for others rather than themselves* — and as a result, the system closes them into a sort of pain cave that is not healthy for them or for anybody. The path for them has closed to such a degree at the end that they continually ask for release from pressure through the use of drugs, mostly.

How can this be turned into something of a better way to incorporate happiness?

The person needs to realize they are not responsible for others. This even includes children, to some degree. If a child has enough food on the table, enough in their accounts to live a happy, fulfilling life, the loving support of their parents and other guardians, this is all children need, not huge bank accounts.

In fact, getting rid of these beliefs about how to raise children well is perhaps the best thing you might ever consider, because you, again, are not responsible for their reality beyond a certain point of providing for their best, healthiest life.

There are other lessons to be learned from being in the public eye. These include saying "no" sometimes. This is a hard thing to do when you're a major celebrity with the brand of being nice to others all the time. It is not fun to be constantly interrupted on the street.

Celebrity has its own rewards, too, but the problem is, how do they say no to people without incurring hatred? They can't. But they need to, so as to say, "I am human." This is something of a loss for someone in this state because they are letting go of the need to be perfect people.

What better way to let go of something than to say, "I'm human, get over it"? The celebrity life is more about this than anything.

FIND THE BETTER ALTERNATIVES

Letting go of the presumed need to please
people is perhaps the most challenging
aspect to being human.

So, you have the purpose of life wrapped up in these few paragraphs about the direct causes of the celebrity's problems, but these are also very applicable to your own situations.

1. **You are not responsible for creating anybody's reality except your own.**

2. **You do not need to be kind all the time, nor live for others' approval.**

These two premises are the best way to move into the areas of expression that we call desires.

The phase in which you would get past these occurs in the grief process as bargaining, as we identified earlier as *accessing alternatives — the act of ensuring you can do better next time.*

What can you do better? "What can you do worse?" might be a better question, as in this case, perhaps you need to remove the layers of "better" in order to be happy. That's where the desires really come into play as helpful means to be happy.

Chapter 7:
Realize Your Desires

The actors in our last chapter might have considered other options to "light their fire" and realize their desires.

They might have said, "I'm going to do this for *me* now, not for *you*." They might have said, "Okay, sue me, I'll be having fun doing this next thing which is (fill in the blank… performing a solo act that I wrote myself…being proud of my work rather than feeling I never quite lived up to my own expectations… being not only rich but sharing my wealth in ways that may not please others…)."

There are myriad ways to address any problem: the point is that you address it.

The acknowledgement of an issue is the most important part of how to address it. This is always in the form of what isn't making you happy. Every time you feel unhappy, it is always something that you can address and realize greater happiness, because *every time you feel bad, it's always something you can change about yourself.*

Take, for example, the path in which you have created for yourself a true friend. Say this true friend has some issue with you that you can't acknowledge. Say you have this friend in your thoughts, and you want to embrace what they are saying, but you can't get past the idea they are wrong about you.

What do you feel? Do you feel badly that you have a friend who tells you what needs to be said? If you do, then you need to look at what's causing you the problem. If you don't, then you will address the problem without feeling badly about anything that occurred during the process of recognizing the issue. *The acknowledgement, therefore, is the first thing.*

The issue may be something great or something small. What is the exact issue? You may need to consider many alternatives. Perhaps you are doing something that is not suitable for others, or you are doing something unsuitable for yourself.

In every case, there's always a golden treasure.

Let your shadow help

Now, in finding the treasure, *you need to do some really serious work.* The shadow self has told you what you need to know. The shadow is what you might think of as your best friend in the world, not because the shadow is kind—

because it is *not* kind—and when you realize that, everything you do that makes you feel badly the shadow will point out to you so that you can address it.

Shadow work is the most important thing
you can do to make yourself happy.

The most important thing about the shadow is that it always points out what you can do to realize your desires.

So let's go back to the point of this conversation, to the person who has found something they have lost. The person with the pointed object in their hand now has realized that the world did not cave in because they lost the pencil, or whatever it is that you can imagine—an acting job, a lover, a friend. The object has found its way back to them. However, in the process, they have not accomplished what they set out to do, such as writing their paper, or finding the next acting job. They may find the thing, but lose something in the process.

Isn't this always how it goes? Again, it's not the *thing* that's lost that's the problem, it's *what it represents to you* that is the real value of the loss.

Take, for example, the actor who has lost a part they wanted because of something else they lost in the process. Does the part really mean so much? Why is that? Because they wanted it, damn it! They *wanted* it.

Then what? Say they lost a friend in the process. What's really at risk here? Is it the loss of the part or the loss of the friend? Maybe both. The point is, when you lose something, you lose the wants that go with it, if you really trust the process.

This is life telling you what you need to let go of. In this, the shadow is the key player, because the shadow will say, "What did you want that friend for anyway? The friend is getting in the way of the part." The friend is not aligning with your wants, in other words.

And what better way to make you pay attention than to lose something and feel the loss, rather than not feeling anything because you're so tied up in your wants?

Do you see how these factors all add up to allow you to let go of what you want and focus instead on your desires? There may not be a better friend than the shadow to point these things out to you.

Take another example to heart. Say that when you found the pencil, you got more friends in the process. What you really needed were the friends.

The shadow that appeared to you in the process—the one who said, "You can't go to everybody in your class to ask for their intel in getting your pencil back, because you will be a laughingstock!"—loudly proclaimed that you have to rely on *who you were in the past* to do what you needed to do, rather than to push you into *who you needed to be.*

"So what?" you may have said to the shadow. "I don't need anyone's approval. My goal is simply to get my desires met."

LET THAT SHIT GO

*The shadow will tell you what you're really afraid of,
then let you sort it out afterwards.*

And what you get are your true desires. You get friendships. You get expressions of love. You get fun. And the shadow has played the most important role in your life—as it always does—because the shadow wants you to let go of any fears you have so as to make yourself feel better about who you are.

Now, in getting there, you need to do some deep soul searching. The reasons for being in the world are to address your fears so you can be happy. Your desires play a big part.

Do what you enjoy!

The desires you have continually urge you to have fun doing what you enjoy doing. Some days are easier than others, but overall, your life has a natural trajectory of lovingkindness, fun, and enjoyment. There's no substitute for these things.

*The reason to control what you can is so that life
can give you spontaneously what you seek.*

This is why we said earlier that the path for you is fraught with magical things that happen for your benefit only. What would you do otherwise to realize the path that you were born to?

In this, your intent plays a major part.

*Your intent is hardwired into your soul
and every molecule in your body.*

The reason for intent is to help you differentiate what you really *don't* need to do with your life from what you really *do* need to do with your life. In this, the promise of fruitful means of employment, service to others in ways that bring you joy, and the effortless means to enjoy every moment of your life will be assured.

The reason is because *the way of spirit—your intent working through you*—is what you were born to follow. If you choose to do so, you gain a great deal of personal satisfaction and sense of purpose about everything that occurs *to* you, as well as *through* you, in your world.

The best self is what you are looking to find in every situation. Sometimes this is not easy to do if you consider how many times your situation calls forth feelings of inadequacy, pain, or any number of emotions that block your desire to move forward. In this, intent can play a huge part in getting you through the grief process.

Trust your emotions

Despite what you think of as your "purpose in life," we want to share what *we* consider the purpose of your life, and that is to enjoy it. Your purpose also helps you dig deeper into yourself when you come across feelings of rejection, fear, and love, for even love can spawn hundreds of conflicting emotions within you.

The fact is that your emotions are extensions of your Personal God—your essence Self—and gauging the depth or direction, or even that you *have* an emotional response to something, is your first clue that your Personal God is trying to get your attention. Sometimes you can even feel the Divine working through you in your emotions.

This is the point: emotions play a big role in helping you to get past what you're dealing with so as to cause a ripple effect into your "Personal God sense." You might call this an extension of your Personal God into you that shows itself through your emotional senses.

When you are hurting, you feel emotion. Why? Because God wants to show you how beautiful you are. You cry because you hurt, you suffer because you have lost something, perhaps, or someone.

Until you realize that emotion is purposeful,
you will not understand the deeper beauty in it.

So if you are suffering, realize this is what makes you human. The deeper depths of your essence Self are holy ground for what comes next: the ultimate source of your comfort, which is in your Personal God.

The ultimate source of your comfort
is in your Personal God.

Now what does this statement—the ultimate source of your comfort is in your Personal God—mean to you? What does it take for you to realize you are loved beyond measure?

Sometimes it is in seeking, as well as finding, some part of your existence that comforts you in any crisis, even those that are brought on by your own actions.

So isn't this the point of an absolute loving God? Wouldn't you think an absolute loving God would do such a thing?

To bring comfort to those who suffer is also what you might consider how you respect everything around you. So why not afford this comfort for yourself? Indeed, because you have not fully learned yet, perhaps, that you deserve it.

Know you are deserving

"The way of spirit" is an artful way to say "it's what you are born to do every day to live life to its fullest."

Sometimes the way will be rocky. Do you realize how many people also suffer along with you on the rocky road of life? Yes, all of them.

Do you realize that you are not the only person who suffers? Sometimes, yes, you do. In fact, when you realize what you have sometimes done that has made others suffer is the point here. Sometimes you have made others suffer through your own ignorance or pain.

LET THAT SHIT GO

What does your loving God do to those who are suffering for any reason? Loves them. And what does it take to deserve this love? *Nothing.*

You always have the love of your Personal God.

Now, you might be thinking, "But Rose, why would any God not punish somebody for doing something that causes another's suffering?" *Because that's how God is.*

God does not punish. You punish yourselves because you realize the mistake has been made. Then you succumb sometimes to so much pain and anguish over your mistake or action that you physically become ill.

So there's no point in believing there's a God who is retributive. You will suffer by yourself if you are guilty about something. In this, you need to realize that guilt is not always what you think it is.

Again, the guilt you often feel is only what we call *artificial guilt.* The true guilt that you feel over things that you've sometimes done out of pain or ignorance is what we call *natural guilt.* This is the way of spirit more than you know, for *making mistakes is part of life.*

Beating yourself up continually for things you've done for which you have already noticed and tried to address so as to be a better person is not what's required. The feelings you have that are natural responses to what you've done are important. But you get so bogged down in needless guilt that you sometimes forget to notice where you do need to address things. This is what causes addiction. We will explain.

Addiction distracts you from changing

The reason for addiction is so very simple that you will not believe it at first: it is to dissuade you from changing. *Addiction is the means to ignore or distract you from potentiating changes.*

The facts about addiction are these:

- You have gone through something terrible.

- You realize you must do some inner work to resolve your issues in order to solve the problem.

- You don't have any reason to look elsewhere for support anymore, because you have exhausted all possible external means of solving your issue.

- You turn to distracting thoughts, emotions, habits, drugs, etc., in order to distract you from doing what you need to do.

Having the faith to solve your problems is
the first step in resolving addiction.

Now, we use the word *faith* in the very basic sense. You don't need to believe in God or Jesus or Buddha to have faith. You only need to believe in *something,* and the best way we can suggest to believe in something is to believe that *you have a purpose for living*. This is true, because you know this deep in your bones. Why would you be born otherwise?

The purpose for your life, therefore, is to find out what really satisfies you, then do it.

This is how the world pushes you into what you desire, which is what you really find satisfying as far as how to be in the world. In this, you've been taught about what you should or should not want, and you have wants that you think will bring you satisfaction, but they won't.

It is only your true desires—those parts of yourself that call forth the beauty and joy in the world—that matter.

The world pushes you into your desires

Let's say that when we left our hero with his pencil problem he was searching for the pencil, could not find it, and finally gave up the chase. The challenge for him, therefore, is to grieve his loss.

Isn't this what you do a thousand times throughout the weeks and years that you live? You are constantly losing things, though you may not recognize the losses at all. You might say, "Well, there goes another person who

I won't be friends with," or you say, "I had really hoped this would turn out this other way and it didn't."

The fact is: you weren't supposed to have that thing. That's where your way of spirit comes in.

When you realize the world wants your best life, you will realize that to lose things is a perfectly natural response to your deep intent: the reason for your birth, life, and eventual death. There's no substitute for finding your intent in life, whether it is as a juggler, barkeep, sand sculptor, or corporate executive.

There's no way you can be happy without discovering and following your path in life.

What better way to find your path than to lose something sometimes? Do you consider that the loss is meant to be? Sometimes you do, and sometimes you don't. When you consider that the loss was meant to be, with the resulting shift of your own internal belief structure you will get a sense that the loss will probably work out fine eventually.

Even if you can't see how that loss was necessary, you can say to yourself, "It will probably work out in time." That's what we suggest you do when you have lost something.

So let's say the child without the pencil is now saying this to himself, "It will probably work out in time." What would you do in his case? Perhaps ask to go buy another pencil, pronto. Perhaps he will look in his book bag for another. Perhaps he will ask to borrow one from a student close to him.

Do you see where we're going with this? What happens is that the world provides something the boy needs in order to be more fulfilled than he would have been if he had not lost the thing in the first place. He makes a new friend. He gets a break he needs from the class to visit the bookstore. He discovers something he had forgotten about in his book bag.

What the world provides is what you *desire*, not always what you *want*. So in responding to grief, you can get a sense that there are better options that you have not considered before.

For example, you might do better without this person you lost, despite how you feel right now. This sounds a bit harsh because you love this person and you are grieving.

But is it so wrong to consider that perhaps you are relieved by their passing and can bloom now in new ways?

Is it so wrong to at least consider this?

What about how you move through your grief?

Can you spend time with others in ways you've not had the chance to before?

Can you find options from those people on how you might proceed in the future?

Can you think that there are ways to get past the notion that you had to have that thing or person to be happy?

Yes you can!

> *This is the thing that most people miss when*
> *they are grieving: life will tell you what*
> *you need to do, you just need to listen.*

Chapter 8: Deal with Desperation and Depression

Now, what about when the circumstances are such that the person who has lost something or someone can't abide by anything that's different in their life? Then the trauma continues until it is resolved by some act of miraculous intervention.

This happens more than you realize. A person who is grieving may be so traumatized by their loss they may reason they are not capable or deserving enough that they consider suicide. They may not want to live anymore.

Bring safety and comfort to the desperately grieving

This is a standard response to great loss and should be considered by anyone in proximity to a desperately grieving person so as to bring safety and comfort.

The problem here is that the path for them may be occluded for too long a time for them to find relief. They may consider suicide. They may consider murder, even. In this, the path will look very rocky and dark. The sunshine of love for them will be the best sort of healing that anyone can provide.

When someone is truly suffering and desperate for solutions, the best thing for them is to help themselves to sunshine in others. However, when the path is too occluded, this is not an answer.

So what do you do? *You give it to them anyway.* You surround them with loving energy. You bring them food. You do *not* say, "You need to look at why you're doing this." *This is not appropriate.* In time, they may become more open to possibilities of how to respond with greater happiness and joy, but if there is any sense they are not open to it, to lecture them is not the best thing in this situation.

The best thing is to just love them. Their faith will come back eventually, even if it is only after they have passed on.

Now does this sound like an odd thing to say? Not at all, if you have read our previous statements about how to navigate the world knowing that you will continue beyond your eventual physical demise.

You know we will say a few more words about this because we have many reasons to say this over and over.

You do not die. You continue to live on after you have been shed of your body.

This is not really an issue if you are happy, but being unhappy makes you consider that somehow you will find relief when your body dies. *But this is not the case.* Although you may find temporary relief from your issues, you will take your issues with you, then find healing in the afterdeath environment, which will help you resolve your issues that you had when you were physical.

In the case of the person who is traumatized by loss, there can be a redemption of faith, but not redemption of sin, because this is not accurate.

The redemption of faith is what a person who is deeply dispirited by loss needs, and if not found, takes the form of depression, which we have touched on earlier but will say more about now.

Depression is supposed to be temporary

Depression is the continual aggravation caused by loss, but it is not supposed to go on forever. It is treatable temporarily by drugs and other forms of comforting chemicals and treatments.

Because you believe that depression is an illness, you take away any hope that people have of ever getting over it. This is not at all accurate.

To say that depression is an illness is to
treat it as something bigger than it is and
to condemn people to a life of pain.

DEAL WITH DESPERATION AND DEPRESSION

Now, we want to express also that desperate people do desperate things in the name of depression. This is another problem with calling depression an illness, because you therefore excuse, in some ways, the actions of others. This is a terrible blight on the United States in particular.

The reasons for this mass hallucination — which is that everybody must be depressed forever — has to do with the beliefs that you can't get better with what you have, that you can't be happy with what you have, and you can never really get what you want because there's always going to be somebody getting in the way of your happiness.

In this, you've produced a giant called Depression that is here to take away every source of joy that you might ever discover. Do you see how this results in the catastrophe that is the medical profession treating you with the drugs that *truly do* take away your joy of living?

So when you consider depression an illness, realize this is a terribly limiting belief that somebody is trying to impress on you for their own profit.

Desperation is the problem, not depression.

The desperation is in finding no way past the anguish of loss. The depression that results from desperation is the temporary phase in which the path becomes clearer.

When the desperation is resolved, the resulting depression is removed.

Some people also have issues that invoke a treason of sorts with regard to how others respond to their desperation. They say, "If everybody would just stop telling me to 'lighten up and be happy,' I would not be so miserable. I would be less miserable than I am because then I would only have my desperation to deal with."

But the problem with this is that you never really have the tools to let go of depression if you don't have some sort of faith that things will work out. That's what people are trying to tell you when you are desperate, or in your terms, depressed. What they are doing is trying to love you into the next phase.

Do you see how this is not an issue, really, but an aversion to faith? It's not *them* who have the problem, it's *you*. So why are you saying they are the ones with the problem if you're desperate for answers?

So when others respond to a desperate person with messages that life can be better in time, it's not a bad thing. They don't mean any harm. It's just that the desperate person is not in a place where they have yet accepted there is a reason for their being, where they can have faith things will work out.

This is perhaps the most important part
of grief work: to help people realize
their life has purpose.

DEAL WITH DESPERATION AND DEPRESSION

Love those who are despairing

Now, we don't want you to tell somebody who is in the pits of despair that life has purpose, because this is not going to help them grieve. The point of grief, as we said, is to move through the emotional problems that are caused by loss and get into a state of recognition of one's Personal God. The Personal God part is only found through gently prodding them towards feeling better through loving them.

You express your Godhood when you love others. They will respond with gratitude. That's all they really need. When they are ready to talk about how they want to feel better, you can say that you know they will, period. You have faith in them, God, etc., when you say only, "I know you will." And you do, because you've found *your* way of spirit.

In spite of what others tell you about how to be a good or better person, you know through your intuition if and how you need to be a better person, and you can be. But ultimately, you need to be a *happier* and *more loving* person.

In this, the spiteful people will say, "You know, I think she needed to lose that thing because she was not a good person."

Do you see how horrible this is? In reality, no one has any reason to judge others this way. *No one calls the shots about who is deserving of what.*

So if there is anybody like this in the chorus of people surrounding the person who is grieving their loss, you have every right to invoke your Personal God and say to them, "I don't believe that anybody deserves to suffer. In fact, my goal here is to help them not suffer as much, if I can."

Leave it at that. Don't argue for deserving or not deserving. There's no reason to, because life does not rest on deserving or not deserving. Life rests on whether or not you are following your way of spirit.

Here are the facts:

- Life is about your finding your own path.

- Life wants you to be happy. Having fun is a huge part of your being happy.

- Life also longs for others who want to help you be happy and vice versa.

- You have reason to be here doing what you love.

- Doing what you love includes having things to offer people to help them grow, too.

- Life is all about service to others, which is not exclusive to your happiness, nor is it exclusive to only those who you may think are somehow less than you.

DEAL WITH DESPERATION AND DEPRESSION

Have fun helping yourself and others

Do you see what a disservice it is to suggest to yourself that service is only what *others* do for you, not what *you* do for others? In this, the propagation of beliefs that "service is only for the servants" is the most destructive belief system you perhaps have in the world.

Be of service to others.

In this, to comfort others with loving thoughts and expressions of faith in them is the best thing you can do for a person who is grieving.

Now, we want to say for the record there's no reason to do anything that you don't really enjoy doing. This seems to be an adverse sort of belief to have if you think that everybody will naturally only be out for what they can get.

This is not the case, for you are truly good beings — deep down, perhaps — but all individuals have the ability, as well as desire, to share what they have. This is not only an issue that needs to be resolved in the world, it needs to be resolved in yourselves.

Life is a series of accidents that you are here to avoid, right? *Wrong.* Life is a series of opportunities that you can take or not take. The life you create for yourself is wonderful, creative, and divine in its ability to provide you what you dearly desire. Life will sometimes throw curve balls at you, as we said, so as to help you move into areas of expression.

If you don't believe that you have the right to be happy, or to have fun, this is where you really need to address whatever beliefs are preventing your happiness. This is what we call the belief work, because your beliefs *do* create your reality.

If you are not having fun all the time, doing what you do to help yourself and others to feel loved and express that love, you're not doing the life thing right.

You need to get better at it.

This seems like a strong statement to make. "Rose, I can't have fun without it costing somebody." Really? It's not like you to say this, because we know you can. We are saying this so you can reconsider what it takes for you to have fun.

Now, in the case of the grieving person, it's not appropriate to point out that life is supposed to be fun.

However, this person may eventually need to decide on a course of action that really is very fun. What prevents them from doing it is often this: they don't know how, or they have been relegated to a role in which they have been taught is to only serve drudgingly, or they do not think they deserve things because they are not worthy, or they can't have fun until all the world's problems are solved.

DEAL WITH DESPERATION AND DEPRESSION

In this, they need to make the connection between what is truly worthy of them and what is not.

This is where the real beauty lies, because you have the sense that worthiness is what the world needs in order to feel alive again.

Know you are worthy

When you project on others what *you* want to have, then tell yourself you're not worthy of what they have, that's why you don't have it after all. You set yourself up for failure.

When you view the world as providing you what you need and desire, *then you really have it.* The world will give you wants, desires, and needs. You just need to want, desire, and need the right things.

Therefore, shifting into a space in which you can see the future as something fun is what you want to work on next.

There's no other solution for despair than looking towards a future that is fun.

The part of you that has a hang-up about this thinks that you don't deserve to have fun because fun is irresponsible. You think that fun is something that longs for itself, however, it is not just this: it also longs for *you*.

When you get tired, when you have pain, when you have predilection towards non-fun, what is there to say except that you're miserable?

You have fun sometimes being in pain, yes. Sometimes you say, "I'm going to feel sorry for myself for a while," and, "I'm going to take my pain out on somebody else." However, these are not highly recommended. In fact, they can make matters much worse, because then you have the added guilt of knowing that you did something that was in conflict, in somewhat egregious ways, even, with somebody's happiness.

You might think that being sorry for yourself
is not an egregious act of violation
against somebody because that person is you,
but you would be wrong.

If you are doing something that makes you feel sorry for yourself, that's not only a violation, that's another problem because you now are into the area of self-deprivation which is not sacred, nor is it in any way recommended.

The self-deception involved with self-deprivation is that you think you're doing something that's wonderful, because look at you, you don't need what you thought you really desired because of various religious beliefs, or because your esteem is not what it should be, or because of how you were taught to think about yourself.

DEAL WITH DESPERATION AND DEPRESSION

However, self-deprivation is not at all the spiritual path we would consider good for you or holy in any way.

> *Deprivation is based entirely on beliefs*
> *that you are not worthy.*

When you are taught that you have original sin, that you are here to suffer, that you are here to exploit others, and you condemn others for their habits or their predilections—that, especially, include fun—then you're doing abnormal things, period.

This is not normal, natural, or spiritual. This is simply your shadow saying that you would rather be doing whatever it takes to be where that person is in ways that would offer you a chance to have fun.

So when you project your shadow on others who are doing what you consider fun, you are saying, "I don't deserve that."

> *This is the number one cause of your suffering:*
> *not recognizing the shadow and what*
> *the shadow can do to help you.*

Chapter 9: Create
Your New Reality

In the beginning of this book was a clue about the shadow and how it works, and that was to say that grief is sometimes caused by looking at what it was that you did that could have been better.

When you can't look at how you can do better, the shadow will step in and cause havoc, insisting that you *were* the perfect person, that you *had no idea*, that you *had to do it because...*, etc. You justify your actions by putting the blame on somebody else.

The shadow will step in to assuage your ego that you had *nothing to do with* the cause of any problem, or that you *did not mean to* do it, when in reality, perhaps you could have done better.

The shadow will tell you that you are wonderful, perfect, and anything that you do that is wrong is surely because of somebody else. *Wrong.*

CREATE YOUR NEW REALITY

*Everything that you create in your reality
is because of you, and you need to realize
this to be truly happy.*

Now what do you say to somebody who has lost an arm to war? You don't say, "Sorry, but you create your reality." This is not the purpose of the teachings that you are now learning.

The reason this is important to stress to you is *that life is very subtle.* There are always things you cannot see with your limited perceptions. Individuals choose things on a much deeper level than you can ever know.

When you criticize somebody for creating their reality wrong, you project your shadow of indifference to the subtlety of life as "spirituality in process."

*You gain nothing from wronging on somebody
for creating their reality. The same holds true for
wronging on self for creating your reality.*

You have no idea why sometimes things happen the way they do because you have a limited perception at the time. However, upon reflection, you can realize much reality creation at work in your very own beliefs.

Your beliefs and reality shift together

In this, the way of spirit calls to you to look at every single belief you have in order to understand what happened and why. You may not get new information, you may not even get full information, but you can look at your own actions to see how you can do better next time.

The cyclical motion of the sun is an example of how you can consider your beliefs and the reasons why something happened.

When mankind was young, they looked to themselves as the center of the Universe. Now your sciences more accurately explain that your earth orbits the sun, and that the Universe is much wider than you'll ever know.

How is this the same as looking at your beliefs? You are not the center of the Universe in the same way you thought, perhaps, when you were living in the times this belief was widely accepted. In that time, the poison of believing that mankind existed "for its own pleasure only" was born.

This is not entirely inaccurate. You can find pleasure in the world. However, there is reciprocity that needs to occur if you are truly being happy.

In this, the "sunshine of love" belief was created as a new way to look at the proximity of the sun—not as a god, not as an essential tool for vegetation primarily—but as a means to realize that the sun shines for everybody.

The sun's history, therefore, has changed. It has turned into less of an orbiting satellite or "one God to rule the Universe" and into more of a realized Self that shines on you as your Personal God. Do you follow? Your God always shines for you. Your God always shines for others, too. Your God has no need to compete with other Gods for your salvation.

If you believe that life is intentional, that life has reasons to sometimes gather itself up to provide you what you need in the world, then you get the sense that the world wants you in it, thriving. The world wants you in it to be happily dozing off in the sunshine, sometimes eating foods that are healthy for you, exposing yourself in ways that feel wonderful, and healing what you need to through the Light of Love.

What better analogy is there than to realize the sun is here for your happiness? It's dark in your world now. There are many people who are suffering. The best you can do is to not suffer for reasons that do not suit you. We'll explain.

Generous doses of love are, as we said, required for those who are suffering. Of course, if someone is hungry, you feed them. If someone is unclothed, you give them your cloak. These are all things that were taught early on, in your childhood.

When you hurt, what do you do? You express your needs, if you know them, as our boy did with his missing pencil. Sometimes the needs go deeper than you can know. That's why expressions of lovingkindness are required, as we've told you.

But when the hurts go so deep, when the darkness is everywhere, when the light is nowhere to be found, what do you do? You pray.

Now, we will say that prayer has maximum value when you do it realizing that all prayers are answered, just not in the way you have learned.

Prayer is intention in action.

When you pray, you set your intention to the things that need healing. Your job. Your body. Your soulful expressions that you don't have going on in your life. When you pray, you say, "I can't do this alone. I need help. Please help me."

Then you think about the problem in ways that require intervention. This intervention is your Personal God who is in full charge of your happiness. They will respond, just not always in ways that you think they will. If you desire the thing, you will get it.

The problem becomes when you want something that you won't really benefit from. That's when you say, "Okay, I will pay attention to what you think is best and I'll not worry about anything else."

Do you see how the very act of expressing your desires is needed?

When you get past what you <u>want</u> and really sink into the love of your Personal God, you will see that most of the time, you have everything you need to have fun.

Having fun is the goal here, as we said. So let this be how you consider the path for you:

You want to have fun, and in doing this work, you let go of what's not fun and realize what is fun.

So when we last left our hero, he was considering the paths of what might fulfill his needs. He was stressed out a bit, thinking about the many paths he could take. He said to himself, "Well, that one may not feel so great" or, "That one might feel wonderful." He felt through it.

Do you see? He does not need to wrong on himself for having a need that requires fulfillment. He does not need to worry that others may perceive him as lacking. He does not even care what the teacher thinks, because she needs to know he's in need of something.

When he realizes that he's in a situation in which he can have fun, he might even say to himself, "I can't believe it! This is so great! I can stand up and say what's on my mind without fear!"

Do you see how that shift slightly to the fun side changes everything?

If he does so, perhaps someone will throw a pencil to him. He might miss, he might not. In any case, what does it matter? He can catch the pencil and proclaim victory. He could miss the pencil entirely and have it end up next to the pretty girl he's been wanting to talk to. He might even say, "I have been wanting to talk to you. Now I have a chance. Would you like to have lunch together sometime?"

Your contrary self loves you no matter what

Now, you may not see how this is applicable to you because you have many very important things to worry about. You have your presentation of self to worry about.

How will others perceive you? Does it really matter? No, because your Personal God loves you no matter if you are short, tall, funny, not funny, cute, not cute, overweight, self-damaging, urine-soaked, having trouble getting work, etc.

Your Personal God loves you no matter what.

In this, you can count on your *contrary self* to pull you out of any jam that you find yourself in.

*Your contrary self is the self inside you
who reminds you that neither you nor life
are supposed to be perfect.*

So what happens when the pencil sails between your outstretched fingers and into the eye of the boy who sits behind you? Do you say, "Oh my god I'm so sorry!" Well, not if you have enough self-esteem to realize that you were not at fault, that it was an accident.

You can express to him, "Can I help you with that?" That's all you need to do. Hopefully there's no damage to be worried about. If so, you get them to a doctor.

Do you follow? *You do what you can do.* You don't wallow in the sense of saying, "I'm so going to hell for that," or, "I'm so clumsy," or, "I'm so... (this or that)." If you think you don't do this, realize you do this more than you know.

And in this, the game of life will always help you by providing somebody in your corner—your contrary self, your Personal God—to always tell you something you need to know.

If the boy who missed the pencil knew about the contrary self, he would be more likely to call on that self to help him in the situation. His contrary self would say something to the effect of, "Well, there goes your 'A'." What would be funny is if you were already a C student. Your contrary self might also say, "It's not in your genes, this catching thing. Maybe you shouldn't go out for captain of the baseball team."

> *It's not that you're in any way flawed, you're just allowing yourself to <u>not</u> be perfect.*

In this, the flaws you think you have are only the places you don't love yourself yet. So when you try to do something and fail, there's no need to wrong on yourself or worry about it. You just don't do it well yet, or perhaps are not called to do it yet.

This is where intent comes into play. The path for you is always going to challenge as well as change you. The path for you will also look out for your best interests. If getting caught with a pencil in your eye is supposed to happen, it will. This is not to say it is desired, but you know, shit happens. And when shit happens, you grieve. You cast about for reasons that it happened, and in this, your intent will say, "It doesn't matter much. We have your back. We essences always have your back."

Now, you may not agree that essence or loving spirits are around you always, but they are. You can let go of any notion that we don't call the shots—we do ultimately— however, you're allowing yourselves as souls in process to *feel into things* rather than *think* all the time.

In this, your intuition is your best way to realize what's going on in any situation. Teamed with the intellect—that you know is sometimes more about proving one's smarts than really using it for good—your intuition is the way to really get down into the depths of the purpose for anything.

The purpose for your eye with the pencil in it may not be realized immediately, because you have pain to deal with, as well as a trip, perhaps, to the doctor's.

But when this has been attended to, when you have done everything in your control to help the situation, that's when you start praying, or meditating, or whatever it is that incorporates the perspective of the sunshine of your Personal God that requires itself to be brought into situations in which you will benefit.

Your essence Self—your Personal God—does not require itself to be involved in everything that you do every day. You're here to learn things, to express things, to sometimes feel badly about things. This all goes into helping you to be more like God, in a sense.

So when you consider how very rapidly you learn things when shit happens repeatedly—for sometimes that's how things go—you can say to yourself, "Wow! I am really creating the potential to gain wisdom here!" as we say.

This is also sometimes expressed as "another frigging growth opportunity," and there's truth in this. For as much as you don't want harmful things to happen, sometimes there's reason for it.

So let's say the boy has caught the pencil with his eye, but does not require any medicine or treatment. "Whew! That was a close one!" he might say.

What you might do in this situation is to say, "I'm so glad I have my (fill in the blank)." In his case, it may be eyesight. If you have a close call, why not say, "I'm so lucky I did not have that happen, and I appreciate that I have (fill in the blank) in the first place"?

But let's say this is a more serious issue, that the pencil did not cause permanent harm, but did cause pain and suffering.

What does this amount to in the big picture? Something needs to be let go of, perhaps the idea that every face is supposed to be perfectly symmetrical, and that the cut on his eyelid will leave a scar, and that's what needs to be resolved.

> *Your facts carry with them a monument's worth of meaning and symbolism that is breathtakingly beautiful.*

It may be something he would connect with in spiritual ways by saying to himself, "I'm beautiful in spite of the scar on my eyelid."

Now, what if ultimately he was to lose his eyesight in that eye or in both eyes? What purpose would there be to that? He would need to have some comfort that perhaps he had not afforded himself. He would get some attention that perhaps he needed. He may try to justify it by saying, "I was not quick enough," but in reality, that's just wronging on self that would not be required for his healing.

He may become someone who has found *purpose* in not having sight in one or both eyes, such as somebody who needs no depth perception in order to do his work, which would include, perhaps, works of artistry that had never been realized before, or as a social justice advocate for the vision impaired, or some other way to express his intent in life, which would be that calling deep inside him that the eye business would allow in ways he would not otherwise consider. He would not be a jet pilot nor somebody who drove a bus, perhaps, but what better way to discover what you love doing than to realize that the things you thought you wanted were not really for you?

CREATE YOUR NEW REALITY

This is how life works. In your case, you may have needed to let go of something important to you—like eyesight or some other thing—which caused you great grief. In this, you need to find out what the purpose was so you can move on.

Loss is always for the best eventually

In spite of how you consider loss, it's always for the best eventually. It's never non-purposeful.

The path is always fraught with terrifying things.

And what better way to respond to that beautiful idea about life than to say, "I'm going to be alright no matter what. I'm going to find ways to have fun. I may be a one-eyed poet who gets his kicks living in a small place that has no sharp, pointy edges, and will have fun knowing that I will always be safe. For I have learned that life lives itself on its own terms. I know, deep down, my world is within me, that I love myself in spite of my supposed flaws, and so does my God, who always loves me even if I can't always love myself."

Now, in this, the boy who missed the pencil will need to do some grief work, too. He has been accidentally implicated in the loss of a person's eye.

What can he do? For one thing, he can realize he was not to blame. This is tough to do because you feel for each other very much. But causing more stress and suffering is not helpful. He needs to let go of the notion that he caused it as soon as possible.

There are many symptoms involved with grief that are based in guilt. One is that you tend to think that you are responsible for creating another person's reality, when the reality is that you really don't have to wrong on self for things that happen to others that you were not really a part of.

If he had somehow inflicted the suffering on the boy by intentionally putting the offending weapon in his eye, then he will have a lot of work to do. He will need to sit down with his Personal God and pray like heck. In doing so, he will find the means to admit his mistake and make amends.

If you have done something to harm somebody, you need to do two things.

One, you need to admit it. This is perhaps the hardest thing to do, because your shadow will tell you it's never your fault, that it's always somebody else's fault.

In this, your contrary self will come to your aid and say, "It's okay. I love you no matter what, and no matter what you did." This is not to excuse your behavior, this is merely to say you have many resources in you to make you a better person.

Two, you will need to find a way to say you're sorry. This is perhaps the most important thing for all of you to realize when you do something that you know caused harm, with or without knowledge.

Saying you're sorry is perhaps the one thing that will bring the world to its knees with acts of devotion and kindness to one another.

To say you're sorry for the past mistakes of your people, to say you're sorry for the world's hurts that you contributed to through pain or ignorance, to say you're sorry to somebody you intentionally or unintentionally harmed, is the best salve you can put on hurting people. And the world is hurting. It's time for mass forgiveness for others' mistakes as well as your own.

In this, you can sense where we're going with this because you know who else forgives everything, don't you? Yes. *Your Personal God.*

To repeat, the path that you chose to follow before you were born was initiated by your Personal God, who you may think of as your soul or essence. Each individual ever born has received a sort of path of heroism they will undertake in their lifetime.

These paths incorporate both sorrow and opportunities for joy. Realize we deliberately said "opportunities for joy" because this is exactly what grief is all about: putting beside oneself the horrors of the world in order to find joy. The path is thorny, rocky, and full of opportunities for joy.

The grief process is about finding how the terrible things can provide joy in ways that you may not have considered before.

For example, you sense there's beauty in death. Why? So that others may live. The path of death is something everyone who ever lived needs to experience.

What about death is beautiful as well? You realize that life is not going to be the same forever. You need to focus on what's good. You need to train yourself to become better, happier people, because if you don't, you will miss the goodness of yourself and the world.

This is where deepest meditation is required:
the ability to look inward in order to discover what's
beautiful in every single moment that you live.

Find your new self

Now, part of death is also about letting go, of course. The path of life is always going to be about letting go.

Why do people have such a hard time letting go? Because they can't imagine life without the things they've lost, or they project a future in which they are continually challenged to do things in ways they've always had to do them, because that's what you've been taught: that you are not supposed to change, that the person you were in high school is who you will always be.

Forgiving oneself is about realizing the need
to let go of who you think you were in
exchange for who you think you will be.

This is the most important thing about grief. In letting go of who you were before the loss, you will see ways to favor the new self—rapidly—in exchange for the thing you lost.

Take the example of the person who has not been able to let go of some papers or news stories because they don't want to forget them.

Now, what happens when they lose these things? They have to collect more. They have to savor each one more than they did before. Or perhaps they realize the magnitude of the reasons they are collecting these sources, for their own inspiration, perhaps. They get closer to each story. They want to exchange the *collecting* for *writing* about the story, or *painting* the story, because they realize how very important the story is.

In this, the path of heroism is in taking up what they wanted to do all along: not just to collect the stories, but to advocate for a cause, or to take up writing, for example, to demonstrate the ideas, or to take up painting. Sometimes you won't be able to see this sort of opportunity until you lose something.

This is the best way to see loss:
as an opportunity.

Why would you not do so? Because *you have lost the meaning of loss.* The loss you feel is not a loss in the physical sense, but a loss in the spiritual sense. You lose so you can let go of the spaces you held this thing in order to exchange it for something else. If you can't find out what to exchange it for, here are some helping guides to see you through the actions involved with seeing loss differently.

How to see loss differently

First, look at loss as a way to get better at winning

When you gain something, you feel *geanius* (we made up this word to describe your innate spiritual wisdom that exists in the genetic codes inherent in your body, which are essence, too). You feel wonderful.

You don't really know why you feel this way, perhaps. Maybe you think you look good in the eyes of others, or that you have a greater sense of your own self-worth. However, winning is never about these. Winning is about your way of spirit. The spiritual path for you provides you what you need.

If you win, you can say, "I don't need to worry about how I do this. I'm good at this. I can pursue this further, if I want."

If you lose, sometimes you need to be a better student of the thing you're doing, or you need to say, "I can't do this well. I don't have to do everything well. I don't want to pursue this." Does this make sense?

You're not supposed to win because you are
trying to prove anything to anybody, including
yourself, in some respects.

CREATE YOUR NEW REALITY

*What you do when you win is to exert the power of
your intent as firmly as possible, then see how it goes.
You are not supposed to be good at everything.*

So if someone says you have to be good at something,
you can say for sure you don't if your essence Self says
otherwise.

**Next, try to compose yourself well every day without the
need to feel attached to any one thing or another.**

You don't need to do anything perfectly well. You
don't need to smile all the time. You don't need to please
others by doing something that you don't feel like doing.

This is perhaps more dangerous than you think,
because when you consider yourself somebody who
needs to please others, you can say for sure this is one
thing you will feel a lot better losing.

*The path for you is not to be popular.
Your path is to do good works in the world.
The path also incorporates fun.
Have fun every day.*

If you're not having fun every day, you can bet there's
something you need to let go of.

The paths of inspiration, of individual excellence — of
group excellence, too — are in spending time with others in
fun ways. If you have lost a community of people who try

their best to support you, then you may need to be part of a different one. Set out to find a church or spiritual community to be part of, if that's what you are drawn to. You can also find ways to connect with a bigger group if you simply choose to partake in whatever it is you're drawn to, which can be part of the grief process itself.

Next, to contemplate loss, say, "What is it that I really need in my life? What can I let go of?"

The *wants* that you have sometimes get in the way of what you truly *desire*. The desires are what you are here to gain, dear ones, not every want you've ever had. So look deeply into your heart to see what will really make you happy.

In fact, the path for you can be considered this: doing what you love. Making a good living at it. Toning your body so you are healthy. Letting go of what you don't need. Having fun with birds of a feather. Taking flight in your way of spirit, supported by the people who love you and work to make you happy, as you do them.

> *Some of you don't have the right people around you. Find them through whatever means necessary.*

This is perhaps the number one problem with depression: you don't know who can help you because you've surrounded yourself with people who are not helping you due to their own insecurities and wants.

Don't let them. Find new friends. Find new journeys. Look into your fun spaces to address your issues as to why you're not happy. Get spiritual and psychological counseling. Do whatever it takes to be glad to be alive. In this, service to others is needed.

You can be happy now

The path for you is wide as well as long. As we said previously, you will not die, ever. You will choose a different path when you check out of this physical reality. You will not be any different except that you will see your life as a wondrous creation.

What better way to spark interest in doing this now than to see your future as happy and fun? You will not do so until you work through your problems, though. The path, though rough sometimes, is necessary for your spiritual development. So if you are considering checking out before your time, *realize this will not help you.*

However, you can look forward to a time when you see the world as wondrous. Why not do so now and skip the bad parts of thinking that you're terrible, or the world is bad, when in reality it's a matter of how you choose to view it?

If you see the world as constantly changing in ways that favor you, you will see that it really is true.

If you see that the world provides you with many beautiful things, and lets you lose the things you need to along the way, what could be better than that?

If in fact you don't see the world this way, *you need to.* So do so.

The path is going to be beautiful as long as you realize that life will give you what you need and take away what you don't.

Respond with love for self, love for others, and love for everything that ever lived.

For you are all that—*you are beauty in action*—and you need simply to focus on what you desire to be and do in the world.

Then do so!

— PRACTICES —

Access Alternatives

This practice helps you break out of closed patterns of thinking to allow other ways to consider something, rather than just what you consider the right or perfect way.

Imagine a room set up for a late-night poker game. There is a table in the center with poker chips, drinks, and whatever munchies you'd like.

Now, allow the alternatives you're considering to drift in as players assembling at the table.

There will be one dominant player, a loud and sassy one who postures quite a bit and wears a funny hat. This player is the most obvious alternative that you are starting with. He is going to ante up many chips. And he is the one you want to take to the bank.

The other players will ante up, too, and provide alternatives that you have not considered. They are your contradictory thoughts, saying, "That's not the winning hand, mine is!" They might say, "Trust us! We represent a beautiful set of probabilities that you may enjoy *much* more than his. For god's sake, why would you trust a guy wearing a hat like *that?!*"

There are potentially infinite numbers of hands—or probabilities—worth considering, and some of them will certainly beat the funny hat player's hand. Each player bets that you will be happier with their alternative. They will also come up with alternatives that you are not yet aware of.

PRACTICES

Now, as you allow your players to inform you of more alternatives, you will notice that one of them has a winning hand. It is perhaps the most wonderful thing you might ever consider, but because you were so distracted by the loud, sassy player attached to the bottom of the hat, you were unable to even see it before.

It doesn't matter which player wins because you are only considering probabilities. You are always the winner. You will always take home all the chips, beers, and munchies, and free yourself of the need to invest in any one player or another.

You are the chips. You are the players. You are all of the probabilities. So it is incumbent upon you to allow anything to happen because you will be the one who experiences it, and you must not consider one set of potentials too strongly because it prevents you from being in the now.

After you have cleared the table, rest in your awareness without giving too much energy to one particular future outcome or another. With practice, you will be able to do this without the need for the poker table, but this is entirely up to you.

We expect you to, in any case, be the winner of every game!

Rest in Rose

To meditate is to relax into a state in which you deeply experience the fealing tone *of essence (Rose invented the word "fealing" to describe "feeling in real ways"). There's no way to do this incorrectly.*

This practice builds on your familiarity with the fealing tone of Rose—which you have experienced reading this book—to help you connect with your own essence. Rose uses the word sonter *to realize breath as your means to connect with your essence.*

Take a few deep breaths—*sonter*—and rest in the beautiful, loving sunshine of essence. When thoughts enter your mind, let them pass like clouds in the sky and return your focus to your breath.

Now, imagine yourself enfolded in Rose's loving arms. You might sense yourself resting in the petals of the softest, deepest, and most beautifully scented rose you can imagine. Rose's fealing tone, and your own essence's fealing tone, will be divinely, deliciously *senxual* (sensual and sexual). Enjoy this fealing for as long as you'd like.

Next, ask your essence Self to speak with you through his or her fealing tone. Your essence may present thoughts, words, or images to help you move into that space. With practice, you will be able to move directly into it. Maintain the state for as long as you can.

Engaging essence in this way is very beneficial to your body, mind, and spirit. We suggest doing this practice whenever you can for whatever length of time is available to you.

PRACTICES

To return to the meditative state throughout your day, just take a few moments to sonter and remind yourself that we are always here for you. Come back to this place whenever you feel the need to speak to us, or to realize rest and lovingkindness.

Identify, Define, and Effortlessly Address your beliefs (IDEA)

Beliefs help shape your physical reality, so you'll want to address limiting ones whenever you find them. This practice builds on the Access Alternatives practice to manage your shadow.

When you feel bad for any reason, notice and **identify** the belief that is blocking your nature to be happy, such as a fear or doubt you may have. The issue will be something you have in the past identified as someone else's problem when it is really yours.

Define how to address the problem. You may need to let go of expectations about things needing to be certain ways in order to be happy, get your wants aligned with your truest desires, assist others in ways that are satisfying for you as well, and myriad things you can do to change the way you think about the issue. Consider the simplest things, and realize that everything in the world has pluses and minuses.

Effortlessly address the beliefs. The idea isn't to remove beliefs, but to allow them to help you realize changes in your thoughts and actions that you can make to get happy. You might take action to repair a problem that you've not acknowledged before was the result of your limitations or beliefs, not someone else's.

PRACTICES

Address and Release Your Fears

This practice builds on the Access Alternatives practice to identify and address your fears.

When you encounter a fear, imagine it is a friend who is trying to help you by bringing an issue to your awareness. If you are going over and over the same thoughts, there is an underlying fear that you need to address.

If the fear indicates something that *is not* in your control, it is because of your ego's insecurity that it is not getting what it wants. In this case, remind your ego self that your essence Self is ultimately in charge and ask for help.

If the fear indicates something that *is* in your control, take action to address it. Then thank your fears for their help, and let them go on their way.

For example, say you fear that an event the following day may not go well. Is there something in your control that you can do, such as prepare for it in a way you hadn't considered before? If so, do. If not, you might ask your essence Self to help you enjoy the day no matter what.

Another example is, you may fear global warming. Since this is not completely in your control, you can request that essence assist. You can also identify what *is* in your control, such as taking actions to live in ways that are harmonious with the earth's ecosystem. This will give you peace of mind that you are doing what you can.

Find Your Intent

The Families of Intent can help connect you with the reason you were born, and help explain the amazing diversity and interdependencies of expression. Each family has an associated color to help identify them in dreams and intuitions, but there are an infinite number of shades and expressions of intent, and each individual is unique.

The way in which you may find your intent is to embrace each kind of family of intent, for they are all you, as you are comprised of the many beautiful intentions of the essential Divine ingredients of your reality. We suggest that you not make the mistake of thinking of these types as groups or tribes that exclude others. This will not be a healthy expression of your Divine Source.

The **Sumari/Speakers (Blue)** are those individuals who do not accept the status quo and make the case in artistry that the world needs changing. The Sumari express themselves in thought and expression through your arts in a variety of media such as books, music, paintings, and more, so as to provide their view of a better world in every way possible. Each meaningful expression is as different as the individual who provides the expression.

The **Ilda/Tellers (Green)** tell their stories through exchanges of information in order to express the differences between cultures, people, and ideas. Ildas have the unique ability to "connect the dots," and this will be a very formidable task in your new world, as the exchange of ideas will impress upon the world the beautiful ideas that may have otherwise been hidden.

The **Tumold/Healers (Indigo)** are the formidable instructors in the ways of medicine, anticipating the needs of individuals with regard to their infirmities, including those of the heart, mind, body, and spirit. The Tumold make people well by encouraging one's own healing capacities, as you know that the only one who can heal you is yourself. *Facilitating healing* would be an accurate description of the Tumold's service to others.

The **Milumet/Rememberers (Red)** are those who lovingly provide inspiration to the world by allowing a deep remembrance of your Divine Source. The Milumet are those individuals who are so interested in the many expressions of life that they do not pay attention to the less important will of others, so as to embrace and communicate, in many quiet ways, the expression of the Divine in every creature. Their expressions are often misunderstood, as they are often contrary to your strive-drive ways. They instill in those who listen the remembrance that you are already exactly where you need to be.

The **Gramada/Formers (Orange)** are those individuals who were born to form things from a variety of sources using a variety of means. They typically come up with the "final" idea that merges together a most impressive array of elements to create something remarkably new, often making revolutionary advancements in your world. Gramada individuals do form their own reality, as you do, and in some ways they form your reality in the mass sense, for their remarkable inventions and operating principles sometimes recreate your world in a most substantial way.

The **Borledim/Nurturers (Pink)** are your wonderful parenting superheroes, but only in the respect that they parent the world. They may also parent children, but the way they do so may in some ways be contradictory to the way you may think an ideal parent would. Nurturers must often wean their children—in the real and metaphorical sense—of their childish ways so as to learn to trust themselves. Borledim make this a very interesting, exciting passion for themselves as well as others, which is a very important thing in your world.

The **Sumafi/Teachers (Grey/Black)** are most interested in *least distortion* with regard to your learning. Sumafi are often very stern and critical teachers because they know you need to interest yourselves in your world in ways that remove the layers of bullshit from your experience. We suggest you keep in mind that the teachers in your lives need to be just, but not nice all the time. Trust yourselves to find out what things you need to learn and from whom, and consider that niceness was never intended to be, in your terms, a required course.

The **Zuli/Imagers (Purple)** are those individuals who serve others through their physical forms. They achieve great things in your sports, dance, in the design of forms such as automobiles, spaceships, and other wonderful creations involving physical structures. The Zuli are in many ways creators of your external physical realities, as their shapes so please you that you may not even have thought that there was a designer involved at all, or that the way in which the designer did so was Divinely inspired. But, of course, it was.

The **Vold/Reformers (Yellow)** sound like a very impressive, many faceted bunch, and they are. The way you know them is through your acts of civil disobedience, your revolutionary exchanges of one form of status quo to another, and your most dramatic activities in regard to world events. They also express their intent using means that may not be as widely known but serve to shake up the status quo in smaller ways: in your families, your religious institutions, in your schools, and so on. The status quo is then replaced by another, more suitable framework.

Discover Your *Belonging-to*

The family of intent you *belong to* is the one that your essence holds in every lifetime. The way you identify the correct family is to trust your deep intuition to tell you, "What way of spirit do I follow at the soul level?" This may come easily to you, because it is the way of spirit that is in you so deeply that you may take it for granted. Also, it is possible to have a combination of family intents, but for now, focus on one or two families.

Then ask your essence Self, "What is my best expression—my easiest way of doing things?" In this, your belonging-to family will become clear to you, as it expresses itself naturally and easily for you in every lifetime. You'll find a comfort level with the family of intent that you choose, as you'll be very familiar with it in inner ways. In this, your family of intent belonging-to is considered your *ease area.*

Discover Your *Aligning-with*

The family of intent you *align with* is the one that you chose to experience in this lifetime. The way to find it is to choose the one or two families of intent that most attract you and yet sometimes cause you trouble. For example, if you have a Borledim/Nurturer alignment, you may find it easy to nurture others but have trouble nurturing yourself.

This is what the alignments are about—*challenge areas* that allow you to investigate other families' unique expressions and help you develop your abilities to their fullest. In this, you'll find a natural aptitude, but it will often have challenges built in. It's as if you get invited to a wonderful party, but there are obstacles along the way and you have trouble getting there.

As with the belonging-to, it is possible to have a combination of aligning-with intents, but for now you can focus on one or two families.

PRACTICES

Dream Practice

Your dreams are a powerful means to understand the nature of your essence Self and help solve any challenge. A nightly dream practice will in time become natural and yield great benefits.

1. **Prepare.** Before sleeping, place an audio recorder or notepad and pen next to your bed. Give yourself the suggestion that your dreams are very important and you wish to remember them. If you have a specific question or problem, ask your essence Self to give you an answer through your dream.

2. **Capture.** When you awake, try not to move, but it's okay if you do. Ask yourself to recall your dreams. If you don't recall any, ask yourself, "What was I just doing?" Then lie quietly. Capture anything you remember. After you rise, writing or typing on your computer in a meditative state may bring out more information. You may also recall your dreams during the day. Pay attention to any small or large image or idea that comes up, and capture it if you can.

3. **Interpret.** You can review your dreams with someone you trust, or use a dream dictionary, but ultimately it is up to you to decide the meaning and value of your dream symbols. You have your own system of symbols and meaning.

ABOUT THE AUTHOR

Joanne Helfrich is an author and channeler whose works promote personal and collective transformation. With the essence of Rose, she provides guidance to help individuals know and embrace their soul's design for expression and fulfillment. She lives in Topanga, California, with her husband and collaborator, Paul M. Helfrich. For more information, visit joannehelfrich.com.

Other books by Joanne Helfrich

The Way of Spirit:
Teachings of Rose

The Afterlife of J.D. Salinger:
A Beautiful Message from Beyond

Afterlives: Firsthand Accounts
of Twenty Notable People

Starman:
My Life and Afterlife

— INDEX —

INDEX

faith, 66, 91–92, 97–98, 100–103

families of intent. *See* intent, Find Your Intent practice

fealing tone, 132

fear, fearlessness, 11–13, 20–23, 26–31, 37, 40–50, 54–55, 67, 71, 88, *See also* Address and Release Your Fears practice

forgiveness, 24, 121–22

fun, 86, 102–7, 112–13, 119, 125–27

future, 6, 10–12, 18–20, 24, 26, 30, 94, 105, 122

geanius, 124

grief, 6, 15–30, 33–41, 46, 56, 61, 71, 76, 101, 121–22
  expiration date, 40
  getting help, 24, 35–36, 61, 66
  giving space for, 40–41
  reaching out to others, 66, 69, 126

guilt, 49–55, 90, 120
  artificial guilt, 51, 53, 60, 90
  natural guilt, 51–53, 90

harm, 26, 38, 42, 100, 117, 120, *See also* violation

health, healing, 1–2, 14, 26, 42–46, 54, 67–69, 73, 77, 79, 97, 111–12, 118, 126, 136
  in the afterdeath environment, 98
  Tumold family of intent, 137

heroic self, heroic journey, 56–69, 121–23

Identify, Define, and Effortlessly Address your Beliefs (IDEA) practice, 134, *See also* beliefs

immortality, 31, 35, *See also* you do not die

inner senses, intuition, 32, 37, 52, 116, 136, 139

intellect, 7, 32, 116

intent, 32–34, 37, 63, 87, 93, 116, 118, 125, *See also* Find Your Intent practice

joy, 10, 12, 18, 30, 40, 41, 61, 72, 87, 92, 97, 99, 121

judgment, discernment, 9, 13

loss, 15, 16, 17, 21–24, 26–29, 33, 34, 38–40, 46, 67, 72, 77
  fear of, 6, 65
  of a loved one, 23, 34–35, 38, 50, 51, 60, 65, 66, 68

medications, 21, 62, 75, 98

www.ingramcontent.com/pod-product-compliance
Lightning Source LLC
Chambersburg PA
CBHW031550040426
42452CB00006B/259